# THE SENSORY TEAM HANDBOOK

**Nancy Mucklow**

*Illustrated by Teena Hartwig and Nancy Mucklow*

Michael Grass House

**The Sensory Team Handbook**

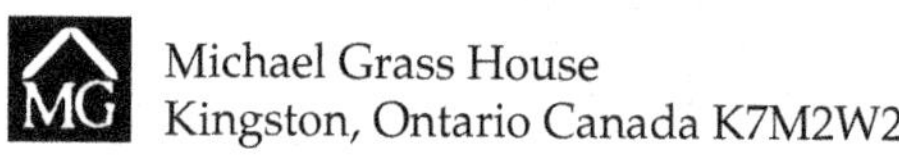



Cover design by Brandon Laird
Illustrations by Teena Hartwig and Nancy Mucklow



The information in this book is true and complete to the best of our knowledge. *The Sensory Team Handbook* is not intended to replace professional occupational therapy or professional diagnosis or advice. The contents are not medical, legal, technical, or therapeutic advice and must not be construed as such. Readers should not use this information to diagnose or treat Sensory Processing Disorder without consulting a qualified medical or educational professional. All descriptions, recommendations, and activity suggestions are made without guarantee on the part of the author. The author disclaims any liability in connection with the use of this information.

**ISBN - 978-0-9811439-2-7**
1. Sensory processing disorder 2. Sensorimotor integration

# ACKNOWLEDGMENTS

*Special thanks to Chris Everdell for her invaluable input and suggestions. Thanks also to Leslie Benecki for her generous help with editing and to Diane Graham and Terri Mauro for their revision suggestions.*

*Thanks as well to Samuel Dunne-Mucklow and Alexander Salterio for their input as readers and to Shane Dunne for his tireless assistance with technical matters.*

# CONTENTS

In fifth grade, I learned that I was different. Before that, school was okay for me. I was **creative**. I was funny too. I used to crack everybody up. The other kids liked me. But that all stopped when school became about being **fast and tough**.

Suddenly, I wasn't cool enough anymore.

I can't tell you how much I **hate** gym class. "Here, everyone, let's throw the ball at Tim and see if he can catch it! Let's play some basketball, and everyone will score except Tim!

"Or how about some dodge ball? Tim can stand in the middle of the firing squad, and we'll all **whip a ball at his head**!" Yeah, it's so much fun!

Sometimes I wish I could make myself **invisible at school**. I never put my hand up, and I always keep my eyes down.

But my teacher always notices me and sends me up to board.  She seems to know when I haven't got a clue what we're doing.

I just stand there, doing nothing. Sometimes I try to write something, but my hands are always shaking. It's like **forever** before she sends me back to my seat!

Remember me? I was the kid in second grade who practically lived in the hall or at the principal's office. I was the one who got kicked out of all the special classes and all the fun games.

The only things I liked were recess and gym class because I could run around. But they were always too **short**. The rest of the day I had to sit doing nothing, till I almost went **crazy!**

# INTRODUCTION

This book is for you.

It's a book for young people who have had hard times at school. You look like everyone else, and you have talents, just like everyone else. But you know that something is in your way that makes life harder for you than for other pre-teens and teens you know.

This book will help you understand those difficulties and get rid of them.

Luckily, the adolescent years are a great time for making changes. Your brain is growing very quickly right now. In fact, it is growing faster now than it has any time since you were born. Things that were impossible for you just a couple of years ago are now possible. So this is a good time to break free of these difficulties.

## What Kind of Difficulties?

Let's take a look at the kinds of difficulties you might have—or might have had in the past. In the quiz box on the next page, check off the items that apply to you.

# What difficulties did you have as a little kid?

- [ ] I was not very good at sports. I never knew where I was supposed to be. I eventually learned to catch and throw a ball, but it took me a lot longer than other kids. I still couldn't keep up with the game like the other kids.
- [ ] I tired out easily. Other kids could keep running and playing, but I needed to sit in the shade.
- [ ] I tripped a lot.
- [ ] I got frustrated a lot. I would try hard to do things but they never turned out the way I planned.
- [ ] I didn't like a lot of foods. My friends all liked them, so I felt kind of left out.
- [ ] I didn't like getting dressed in the morning.
- [ ] I couldn't stand it when someone started talking to me while I was doing something else. I couldn't concentrate on both things. Usually, I blew up.
- [ ] I was afraid of a lot of things that other kids weren't afraid of.
- [ ] I hated the feel of lots of kinds of clothing. I especially hated the tags on shirt collars.
- [ ] I used to do certain activities over and over again, like spinning, swinging, or bouncing.
- [ ] I hated getting my hair or nails cut.
- [ ] I hated taking showers and washing my hair. The feel of water on my face made me feel weird.
- [ ] I felt sick to my stomach doing certain kinds of movements, like twirling. Other movements, like going upstairs quickly, made me feel nervous.
- [ ] I hated surprises and changes. I liked things to always be the same.
- [ ] I got angry a lot. People still tell me I overreact to simple things.
- [ ] I never felt safe.

Most people check off at least a few of these items. But maybe you have checked off a lot of them. If you have, then this book is for you.

## Your Master Electrical System

Let's look at your personal electrical system—your brain and nerves.

Many people think of human beings as having a brain and a body. But we don't, really—we have a brain-body. Our brains and bodies are so completely blended together that we can't really talk about them separately.

Most people have at least a few difficulties getting all the parts of their brain-body to work together properly. But some people whose brain-bodies don't work together smoothly have what is called a **sensory processing disorder**:

> **Sensory** *means about the senses—hearing, seeing, touching, tasting, smelling, and moving.*
>
> **Processing** *means understanding and interpreting.*

*Sensory processing disorder* means that your brain can't understand and interpret some of your senses. We could say they aren't well *co-ordinated* or not well *integrated* together. Sensory processing disorder is not necessarily a permanent thing. There are ways to reduce it or even get rid of it.

Think of a **house with old electrical wires**. Some of these wires short and spark, some are frayed and weak, and some aren't connected. When you plug in the toaster, all the lights flicker. When turn on the television, the fridge turns off. And sometimes, you end up blowing a fuse. The wires are all there, but there are problems with the connections.

Yet an **electrician** can come by and repair all these electrical wires so that the house works smoothly again.

Sensory processing disorder is like this wiring that needs an electrician's help. The brain-body needs rewiring so that everything can work together.

It takes some time—and a lot of work. Rewiring requires changes in your life. But in the end, you'll have a more relaxed and happy self. You won't feel tense and anxious all the time. You won't feel like hiding from others. And you'll be able to think clearly and move smoothly and confidently.

You might be thinking: "I don't need to change. I'm tired of people telling me what to do. I want everyone to just leave me alone."

A lot of young people with sensory processing difficulties say they just want to be left alone. But being alone is kind of lonely. People need to have friends and be able to participate in activities. Try this quiz.

## What are your goals?

- ☐ I want to become good at at least one sport.
- ☐ I want to feel happy and safe.
- ☐ I want to feel relaxed, not nervous and anxious.
- ☐ I want to have a girlfriend/boyfriend some day.
- ☐ I want to be able to join in activities with others.
- ☐ I want to feel that I belong.
- ☐ I want to really like myself.
- ☐ I want to have control over my body.
- ☐ I want to be calm and confident.
- ☐ I want to be able to do things without feeling clumsy or uncomfortable.
- ☐ I want to be able to fit in with others my age.
- ☐ I want to feel good.

Most of these goals have to do with happiness and feeling good. By reading this book and trying out the ideas, you can start working on these goals. You can think of the ideas this book as a set of tools to help you fix these difficulties.

Now, if you're ready, let's start learning about the truly amazing brain-body network you have and about the power you have over it.

# Notes

# 1
# YOUR BRAIN-BODY

This is a brain.

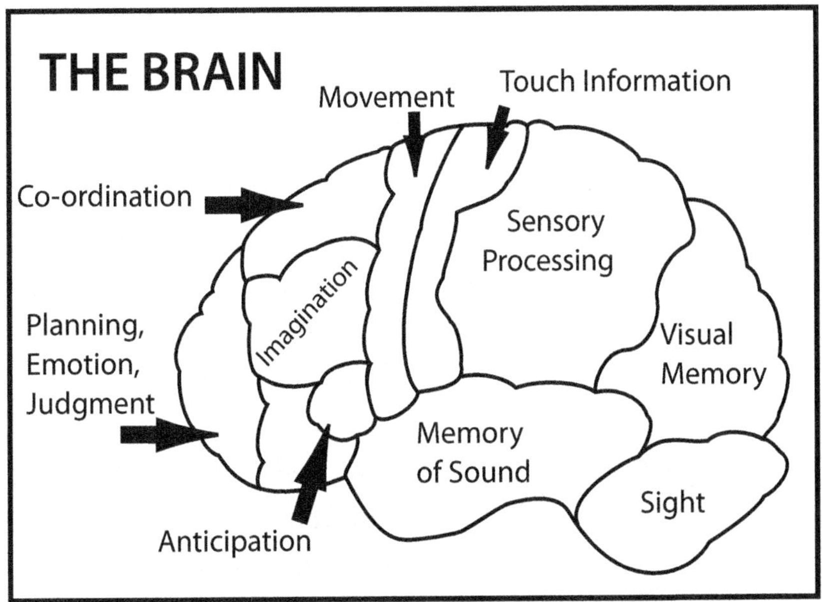


Each part has a different set of jobs to do. One takes care of co-ordination, and another takes care of planning, emotion, and judgment. Other parts control the actions of certain parts of the body, such as the eyes and ears.

What's great about the human brain is that each part is specialized. These specialized parts are all attached to each other, as well as to the rest of your body. They all have to work together to keep your body running smoothly.

## Your Ancient Brain

You can think of your brain as layers of brain evolution. Over millions of years, the human brain has grown from the small brain of our pre-human ancestors to our big modern brain—to allow us to do more and more complex tasks.

But deep inside our big brain, that wild, primitive brain is still there. Its job is still the same: to take in simple information from the world around us and translate it instantly into actions for survival.

The main survival action is the **fight-or-flight response**. If something frightens you, the ancient brain makes you run, scream, hit, or panic, before you even realize what you are doing. It is a very powerful part of the brain, more powerful than the thinking part of our brain.

But like all the other parts of your brain, your ancient brain can be trained not to over- or under-react to the world around you. Its best teacher is hard physical work. Movement, activity, and stimulation keep your ancient brain calm, alert, and focused.

Sitting in front of a computer or at a school desk may help your modern brain to learn, but it doesn't do anything for your ancient brain.

## Your Brain Train System

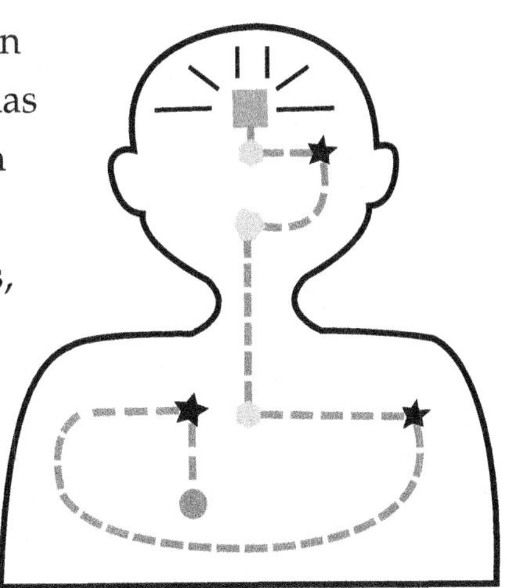

You can also think of the brain as a **train station**. The brain has to manage all the information "trains" coming from the body—such as sights, sounds, smells, tastes, textures, and movement.

It has to bring them to the right brain platforms, connect them with other incoming trains, let some messages off to stay in the brain, and send other messages back to the body.

But your brain is not just a train station. It's also an **airport** at the same time—because it also has to deal with messages from inside your brain too—from your memory, imagination, emotions, and instincts.

Everything is coming in at once from all directions! If one part is too fast or too slow—or too strong or too weak—then these messages won't connect.

### Did you know?

*The brain has the texture of pudding. In a young teen, it's about the size of a small coconut.*

## Your Central Nervous System

The system of railways that attach your brain to your body is called the **central nervous system**. Long nerve cells form bridges between each other so that one body part can communicate with the brain and with other body parts. These links and pathways are called **nerve networks**.

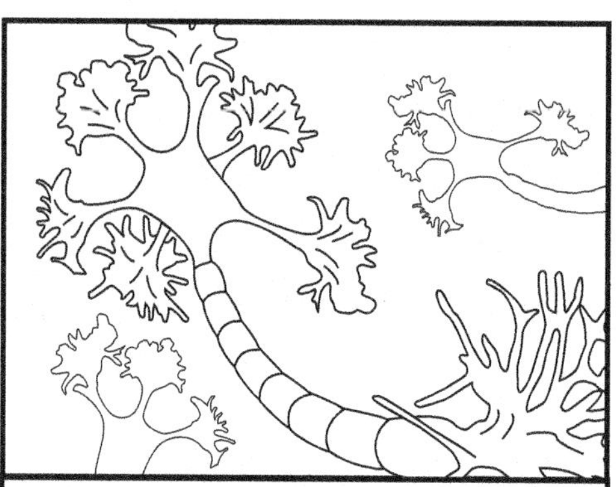

*Nerve cells look like tubes with branching ends. When you practice a new skill, the branching ends reach out to connect with other nerves. Once they connect, you have a new nerve network for performing that skill.*

You have been building up your nerve networks since before you were born. Each nerve network is a message route for one particular skill. When you practice that skill over and over, you coat the nerve pathways—kind of like adding layers of pavement to a road. The more you pave it, the stronger the network becomes, and the more easily messages can ride over the network. Once a network is strong, you will find it easy to do that task.

**Did you know?**

*Nerves receive sensation through specialized receptor cells, which convert them into electricity and send them to areas of the brain.*

## Learning New Skills

Learning new skills is difficult for the brain. It has to understand what the body is trying to do. Then, it has to figure out which sensations and message from the body are important for this new task and which ones aren't. Focusing on the wrong information will confuse your brain, and it will send the wrong instructions back to your body.

Basically, your brain-body gets better at doing tasks that you do often. The more you exercise your nerve networks, the more you teach your brain-body how to handle the sensations and messages. The stronger the nerve pathways, the stronger you become—and the better able to learn new skills and adapt to new situations.

## Brain Train Crashes

Brain train crashes happen when the timing of the messages is off, or where the nerve networks are rough and weak. The brain has a tiny fraction of a second to respond to most situations. There's no time to think. If nerve networks aren't strong and solid, or the information isn't on time, then messages can get derailed or mixed up.

Here are some examples of typical brain train crashes:

**Right doesn't co-ordinate with left:**
Your brain can't tell exactly what your left and right hands are doing, so it doesn't match their actions. You end up pulling too hard with one hand (such as rowing in a circle).

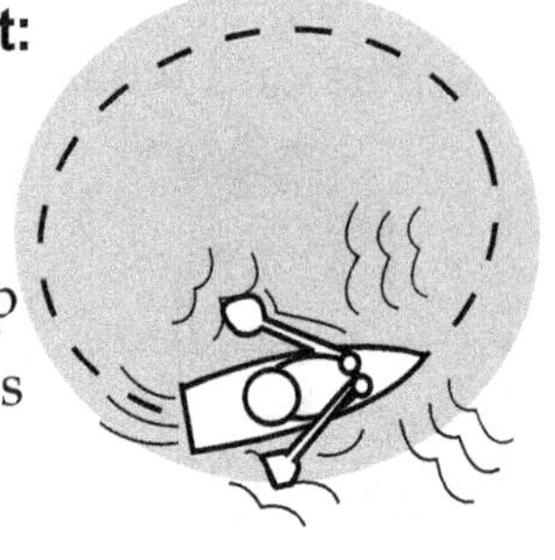

**Confusion crossing your middle:**
The left side of your brain can't time information with the right side of your brain. You can't control movements when your hands or feet cross the middle of your body into the other side's space (such as in a backhand swing in tennis).

**Too much information:**
Your brain receives messages too strongly. If these messages are coming with speed and force (such as a loud or sudden noise), they crash into the brain. Your brain will react with alarm.

### Too little information:

Your brain can't hear small, quiet messages from your body. If you are sitting still, your brain might start to wonder where your body is. Your brain starts telling the body to deliver more stronger messages. You respond by fidgeting and bouncing.

Sometimes the brain becomes afraid because it can't shut out unpleasant or confusing sounds, sights, textures, feelings, and tastes. This can make you feel **anxious**. When you are anxious, you don't feel safe. Sometimes you even feel panicky. Other times you can become obsessive about keeping everything the same all the time so that there are no surprises. Having too much anxiety can make you feel unhappy and afraid even when nothing bad is happening.

But when you strengthen your nerve networks, you will feel safer, and this anxiety will eventually fade away.

**Did you know?**

*Brain messages can travel up to 270 miles per hour (435 km per hour) — the speed of an F1 tornado.*

# ★ FIRST DAY OF HIGH SCHOOL ★

THERE'S SO MUCH TO GET USED TO... **CROWDS JOSTLING** AND **PUSHING,** EVERYBODY **YACKING** AND **YELLING, LOCKERS SLAMMING** AND **BANGING,** TEACHERS LOOKING **MEAN...**

## Building Up from the Basement

You can think of the brain-body as a **house** that is **you**.The **basement** of your house is your **senses**—sight, hearing, taste, smell, touch, muscles, and gravity. To have a strong brain-body, you need strong nerve networks in your basement.

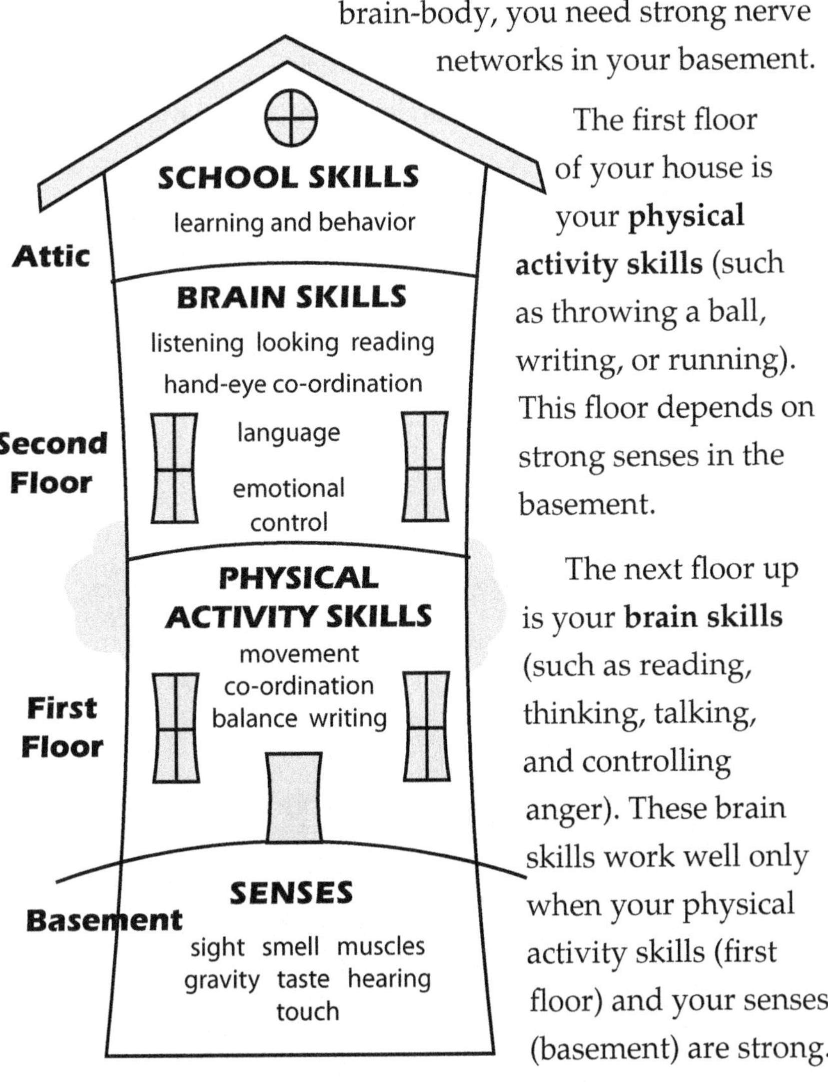


The first floor of your house is your **physical activity skills** (such as throwing a ball, writing, or running). This floor depends on strong senses in the basement.

The next floor up is your **brain skills** (such as reading, thinking, talking, and controlling anger). These brain skills work well only when your physical activity skills (first floor) and your senses (basement) are strong.

All of these floors support the **attic** of your brain-body house. The top of the house is your **school skills**. School learning and social behavior depend on your brain skills, which depend on your physical activity skills, which depend on a foundation of strong senses.

Why do learning and behavior at the top of the house depend on strong nerve networks all the way down in the basement? It comes down to safety. Only when you feel that your house is safe and solid will you want to climb up to the roof.

**Did you know?**

*Animals deprived of sensory stimulation do not develop normally. This is how we know that people and animals need sensory stimulation for growth.*

# Review The Brain-body

- The brain and body work together so closely that they really can't be talked about separately.

- Messages move between the brain and the body through **nerve networks**. You build nerve networks every time you learn a new skill.

- When you practice a skill, you strengthen the nerve network. The messages then move faster and more accurately to and from the brain.

- When nerve networks aren't strong, information doesn't reach your brain. Messages are too late or too weak. Or they may be so strong that they are painful. The brain gets confused and can't control the body properly.

- **Anxiety** can result from a confused brain-body. Anxiety is constant fear and worry.

- If you think of your brain-body as a house, then your **senses** are the **basement**. They are the foundation for all your physical activities, brain skills, and school skills.

# Notes

# 2
# YOUR SEVEN SENSES

Your brain-body has seven senses. You probably know about the five feeling senses:

- **sight,** located in the eyes
- **hearing,** located in the ears
- **smell,** located in the nose
- **taste,** located in the mouth
- **touch,** located in the skin

Less well known are the two movement senses:

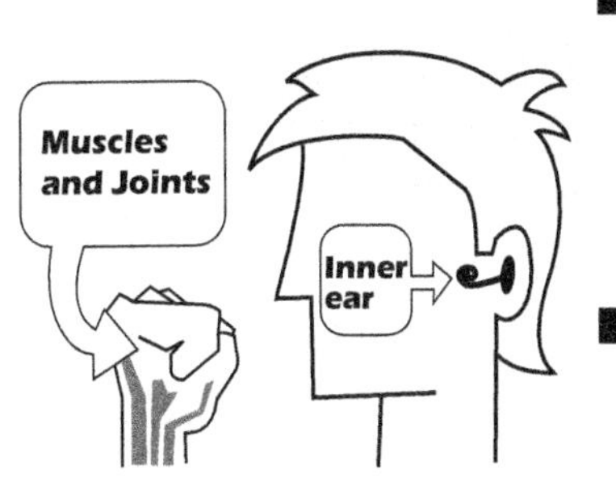


- **gravity,** located in the inner ear (sometimes called the *vestibular* [ves-TI-byoo-ler] *sense*)
- **muscles,** located in the muscles and joints (sometimes called the *proprioceptive* [pro-pree-o-SEP-tiv] *sense*)

Each of these senses is made up of body parts and nerve networks linking to the brain. Since these senses are part of your basement, their nerve networks to the brain need to be very solid. Problems occur when the links between the senses and the brain are shaky.

## Your Volume Control

Just like headphones, your nerve networks have a volume level. If music is too soft or too loud, then you can't listen to it. You strain to hear it, or you pull off the headphones in pain. The same is true for your senses.

- If the volume is **too low**, then your nerve networks are **under-sensitive.** Your brain-body can't feel things much, and you want to turn the volume up. This can make you feel zoned out, or irritable and bouncy.
- If the volume is **too high**, then your nerve networks are **over-sensitive**. Your brain-body feels everything too much and you want to turn the volume down. This can make you feel anxious and afraid.

Over-sensitivity and under-sensitivity are a big part of sensory processing. The same person can have both under-sensitive and over-sensitive senses.

If you have had over-sensitive or under-sensitive senses all your life, then you have probably learned ways to cope with these problems. For example, if your senses of hearing and gravity are over-sensitive, you probably don't go to movies because of the loudness, darkness, and dizzying action. If your sense of taste is under-sensitive, you probably put salt and spicy sauces on your food so you can taste it.

## Sensation Avoiders

People with lots of over-sensitive senses avoid feeling things. They arrange their lives to protect themselves from feeling too much. We can call these people **sensation avoiders**.

Sensation avoiders hate surprises. They plan their day so that they don't have to deal with noisy traffic, cold rain, bustling crowds, scratchy clothes, and strong tastes. If you have over-sensitive senses, you might have already found ways of protecting yourself from sensations you don't like.

### Did you know?

*Animal senses are different from human senses. A buzzard can see a mouse from a height of 15,000 feet (4,600 m). Most fish are color-blind. And bees have a special sense for detecting magnetic fields.*

## Do you avoid sensation?

- ☐ I stay away from situations if I think there might be loud noises, bright lights, and strong tastes and smells.
- ☐ I like eating the same types of foods all the time.
- ☐ I like quiet places. I avoid crowds and places where I might get jostled around.
- ☐ I avoid exercise because it creates too many feelings (like being hot and sweaty, having sore muscles, and being out of breath). Besides, I don't want to fall and get hurt.
- ☐ I use music headphones or videogames to shut out the world.
- ☐ I like having clean hands.
- ☐ I dislike going barefoot outside.
- ☐ I don't like bright, sunny days.
- ☐ I dislike going up and down stairs, elevators, or escalators.
- ☐ I find the glare of a TV or computer monitor too bright, so I avoid using them.

### Sensation Seekers

**Sensation seekers** are the opposite of sensation avoiders. They have lots of under-sensitive senses, so they crave sensation and want lots of it. Sensation-seeking makes people daring, bouncy, and sometimes fearless. It can even lead to risky and dangerous behavior.

Sensation seekers crave sensation. They like to smash and crash into things. They like loud music, high-action movies, and bright lights. If you have under-sensitive senses, you might have a tendency to move, yell, jump around... and drive people crazy.

## Do you seek sensation?

- ☐ I seek out thrills, like going on the scariest rides at the fair.
- ☐ I get in trouble at school for being disruptive.
- ☐ I often work on two or more activities at the same time.
- ☐ I like being barefoot. In fact, I sometimes wear sandals in the winter.
- ☐ I like food that is very spicy or very sour.
- ☐ I don't like quiet activities.
- ☐ I like to do adventure activities that are risky.
- ☐ I like being in places with loud music, bright lights, and lots of hustle and bustle.
- ☐ I often act without thinking.

Remember: people often have a combination of over- and under-sensitive senses. This means a person can be a sensation seeker in one sense and a sensation avoider in another. If you checked off a few answers in both quiz boxes, then you probably have some over-sensitive and some under-sensitive senses.

# SENSATION SEEKER, SENSATION AVOIDER

I **HATE** SPICY FOOD LIKE PIZZA, CHILI AND BARBECUE SAUCE.

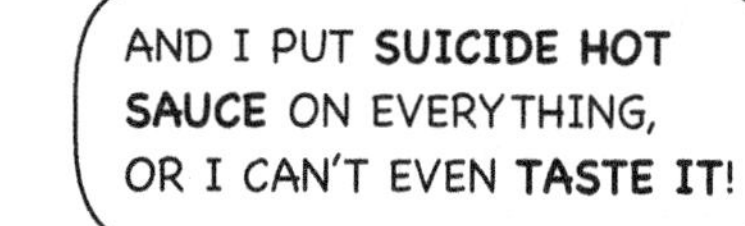

I ALMOST **FELL ASLEEP** IN ENGLISH CLASS TODAY DURING FREE READING TIME. DID YOU?

## Your Sensory Mood

Besides volume control, your senses can have difficulties with **moods**. When senses are in a bad mood, they just don't want to co-operate with you. Then they put *you* into a bad mood!

### Your Senses in a Grouchy Mood

If your senses aren't getting enough activity or stimulation, your nerve networks can go to sleep. Then your brain-body doesn't know what is going on. It can't deal with anything new or unexpected (or boring). Your senses put your whole brain-body in a **grouchy mood**.

THIS IS BORING!
I HATE EVERYTHING!
EVERYTHING SUCKS!

Here are some of the signs that your brain-body is grouchy:

- You feel down, like a car that has run out of gas.
- You feel floppy and tired.
- You feel bored.
- You feel nervous or worried.
- You feel angry or unable to enjoy anything.
- You feel depressed and think everything is all your fault.
- You feel you can't cope with little problems.
- You feel like growling or yelling instead of talking.
- You feel like spoiling everything for everyone else.
- You are unable to get yourself into a nicer mood.

A brain-body in a grouchy mood won't feel like doing anything to get out of the grouchy mood. It'll just want to slump further and further into its grouchiness.

## Your Senses in a Crazy Mood

Sometimes your senses do the opposite—they get too much activity and stimulation. If your nerve networks can't control all the noise and activity, this can put your brain-body in a **crazy mood.**

YAHOO!
THIS IS FUN!
I CAN'T
STOP!

These are some of the signs of a crazy mood:

- You feel like a toy that's been wound up and let go.
- You feel bouncy and silly. You are overjoyed about everything.
- You act wild.
- You talk loud.
- You move faster and faster.
- You feel like yelling and interrupting instead of talking normally.
- You ignore problems as if they don't matter.
- You end up breaking things.
- You make everyone else angry at you.
- You feel unable to stop yourself, as if your "brakes" don't work anymore.

A brain-body in a crazy mood won't want to do anything about it. It won't care about anything except going faster and faster and crazier and crazier.

The best way to get control over these grouchy and crazy moods is to give your senses what they need. You can use the ideas in these chapters to calm these moods.

## Your Senses in Your Growing Body

To make matters even more difficult, during the pre-teen and early teen years, your body is **growing**. You are suddenly taller. Your arms and legs are longer. Your feet and hands are growing too. It's as if you suddenly have a brand new body—one that is changing almost daily.

Your brain takes a while to learn how to control this bigger, taller body. You will probably feel unco-ordinated a lot of the time.

If some of your senses are over-sensitive, you will feel this unco-ordination more strongly than other people. You may end up believing that you are more clumsy than you really are. If some of your senses are under-sensitive, you will not feel this unco-ordination enough. You may end up tripping and bumping into things because your brain isn't sure where all your body parts are.

The best way to take charge of this new body is to keep retraining your nerve networks. If your nerve networks learn to communicate quickly and accurately about your new body, then you will feel more comfortable.

**Did you know?**

*Physical work and strength training in the early teen years creates stronger bones for life.*

## Your Brain-Body as a Team

Think of your brain-body as a **sports team**. Your senses, nerve networks, and brain are all **players on the team**.

### The Dream Team

If you are fantastically lucky, your team is full of excellent players with great instincts and quick reactions. Even without practice and even without a coach, this dream team could win just about any game.

### The Real-life Team

But there's a reason why dream teams are called "dream" teams. Most school sports teams are made up of a mix of good, average, and not-so-great players. Some players know all the rules and plays, and some don't know any of them. Some throw the ball perfectly, others throw it too hard, and some can't throw it at all.

Imagine if some players don't speak the same language as other players, so they can't call things to each other.

And what if there were no coach?

No practices?

How would anybody know what to do in a game?

*Every time we learn anything, we change the blood flow, chemistry, and connections in our brains.*

## Team Practices

If this sports team wanted to win anything, it would have to get out on the field and practice every day. For example, these players would need to

- learn how each player plays
- find ways to work with each other's strengths and weaknesses
- practice plays until everyone can do them together effortlessly
- learn to read each other's signals
- get in shape
- designate a coach

At first, some players might complain. But after a little training, the whole team would feel a new smoothness and strength to their playing, and they'd come to like it. In time, that team would be ready to play in the big league.

## Your Sensory Team

Your senses are like that average team. Some of your senses are strong players, and some are weak. Some throw messages to the brain too hard, and others throw them too gently. Some parts of your body can't communicate with the brain and don't know what other parts are doing.

Your senses need to come together as a team. Your brain-body needs to

- learn how each sense feels things
- find ways to work with each sense's strengths and weaknesses
- practice actions until all your senses can do them together effortlessly
- teach your senses to read the signals of other senses
- get all your nerve networks in shape

## Coaching the Team

Most of all, your sensory team is going to need a **coach**. It needs someone to plan the practices, make the decisions, call the shots, and keep all the senses doing their part. And it needs someone to recognize when the team is in a grouchy mood or a crazy mood and get them out of that mood so that they can get to work.

*How about you?*

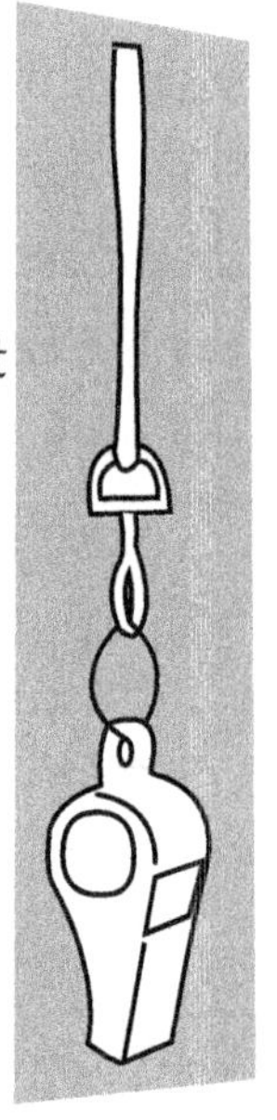

You can be your own coach. This book provides all the information you need to become a great coach for your brain-body team. Each chapter gives information about one sense or group of senses so that you can understand what kind of difficulties it might be having. Then it gives you suggestions for practice activities to make them stronger:

- Some of the suggestions are for **team practices**—activity sessions that you do two or three times per week.
- Some are for **daily warm-ups** to keep your team alert and ready for action.
- And some are for **one-minute practices** that will give your senses a quick wake-up—just when they need it.

So the coaching job is yours. After all, it's your brain-body. You are the best-qualified person to be in charge!

Some people find it hard to be their own coach. If you find you need help, consider finding yourself a coach. Most communities have **occupational therapists** who are trained to help you organize a brain-body practice. They can help you coach your team until you feel confident about taking over the job yourself.

## How to Be a Good Coach for Your Sensory Team

- Listen to your body before, during, and after each activity. Notice what makes you feel better. **A good coach always listens to the team**.
- Check in on your body throughout the day. Are you less irritable, better co-ordinated, more calm? **A good coach checks in on the players**.
- Figure out what combinations of activities work for you. **A good coach modifies the practice to fit the team**.
- Be willing to change. **A good coach is always ready to try something new**.

## Review
# The Seven Senses

- You have five feeling senses: **sight, hearing, smell, taste, and touch.** You have two movement senses: **the gravity sense** and **the muscle sense**.
- The nerve networks for your senses can be **over-sensitive** or **under-sensitive**. Over-sensitive nerve networks avoid sensation. Under-sensitive nerve networks seek sensation.
- If your senses don't get enough activity and stimulation, your nerve networks can go to sleep. Your brain-body ends up in a **grouchy mood**.
- If your senses get too much activity and stimulation, your nerve networks might not be able to control it. Your brain-body ends up in a **crazy mood**.
- Physical growth and brain development in the teen years make control over the senses even more challenging.
- For the brain-body to work well, the senses, nerve networks, and brain have to work like a **team**. They have to learn to co-ordinate what they do so that they don't drop the ball.
- **Regular team practices** can strengthen your senses and your nerve networks.

## Questions to Consider

**1. I hate exercise. Should I do activities and exercises if they make me feel worse, not better?**

If activities make you feel bad, then it makes sense that you don't enjoy them. But maybe your nerve networks aren't strong enough yet for certain activities. They may need more "paving" first. If you can do a little team practice every day, then your nerve networks will become stronger and more used to the feel of movement.

Other answers:

________________________________________

________________________________________

________________________________________

**2. I don't want to spend all my time doing activities. Why not just do what I like to do?**

Everybody needs to do the things they like to do. If you find you don't enjoy activities, then start with just 15 minutes twice a week. After a while, you might find you start to enjoy them and want to do more.

Other answers:

________________________________________

________________________________________

________________________________________

**3. Why do I have these sensory processing problems? How come my friends don't?**

Nobody's brain-body is perfect. Everybody has things they have to deal with. These are yours. But the great thing about sensory problems is that with a little brain-body coaching, you can make these problems get better. Some might even disappear completely.

Other answers:

______________________________________________

______________________________________________

______________________________________________

**4. At the end of the day when I come home from school, I don't feel like doing anything. I just want to play computer games or read by myself.**

A lot of people need a bit of quiet time at the end of the day. If you do, then you should make sure you get it. But if you sit still for a long time, then you will feel worse, not better. By supper time, you may end up feeling grouchy. That's your brain-body trying to tell you that it wants movement and activity. So activities after school are important for your brain-body.

Other answers:

______________________________________________

______________________________________________

______________________________________________

# Notes

# Notes

# 3
# YOUR GRAVITY SENSE

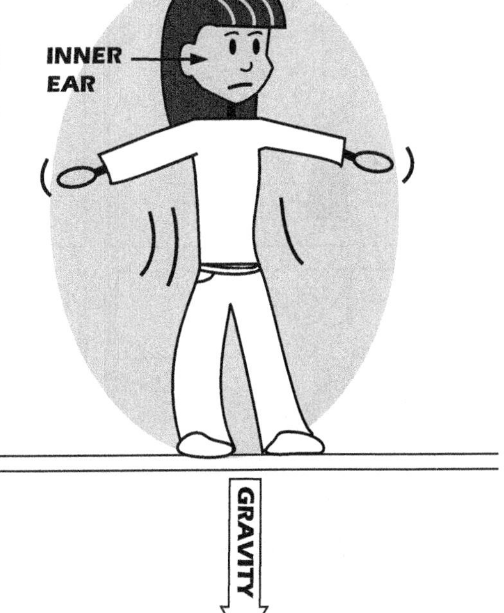


You have two movement senses. One is the *gravity sense*, and the other is the *muscle sense*. This chapter looks at the first of these two movement senses—the **gravity sense**.

The gravity sense is your body's sense of **balance**. Sensors in your **inner ear** feel Earth's gravity and help keep you upright and steady.

The gravity sense is a reflex that can save your life:

- It tells you the difference between dangerous movement and safe movement.
- It warns you to put out an arm or grab onto a railing when your balance isn't right.
- It helps you move smoothly and safely when you are rolling, jumping, and diving.

# BALANCE ROCKS

## Did you know?

*Your inner ear is a labyrinth filled with liquid. The liquid moves when your head moves. The labyrinth walls feel how the liquid is moving. The walls then send instant messages to the brain about your balance and position.*

When the gravity sense is a strong player on your brain-body team, then

- you have a good sense of balance.
- you can move smoothly and confidently.
- your brain understands the gravity messages it receives and makes good decisions about how to move the body to keep balance.
- your brain makes sure your muscles respond just right so that you don't under-react to a situation (failing to dodge a ball) or over-react to it (dodging the ball so hard that you fall over).

When the gravity sense is a good team player, your brain-body knows which body parts are moving and how everything relates to the hard ground below. But when the gravity sense has not had enough practice, it can't control your balance, and you won't feel good.

## Over-sensitivity and Under-sensitivity

Your gravity sense needs to be a strong player on your brain-body team. When it isn't, it's either **over-sensitive** or **under-sensitive**.

**Over-sensitive Gravity Sense:** The volume is **too high**. You feel shifts in movement and balance too much, and your brain reacts too strongly. Your inner ear sends alarm signals to your brain whenever you move, even if you are not at risk of falling.

**Under-sensitive Gravity Sense**: The volume is **too low**. You barely feel shifts in movements and balance, and your brain is never really aware when you are losing balance. Your inner ear craves information about the body's position, so it makes you move, fidget, swing, bounce, and rock.

## Do you have difficulties with gravity?

**Part A**

- ☐ I worry about safety. I don't feel very safe.
- ☐ It took me a long time to get used to riding a bicycle.
- ☐ I feel awkward and unco-ordinated and tend to fall a lot.

**Part B**

- ☐ I dislike intense movement, such as sliding, swinging, and jumping.
- ☐ I have a fear of heights.
- ☐ I dislike elevators or escalators. I prefer stairs.
- ☐ Whenever I try something new or go somewhere new, I feel anxious that I'm going to fall. I am always very cautious.
- ☐ I don't like tipping my head, such as leaning from side to side or washing my hair in a sink.
- ☐ I get carsick faster than everybody else.
- ☐ I don't like moving. It doesn't feel safe. I'm very cautious when I move.
- ☐ People say I overreact (e.g., cry out, yell) when I have to do movements I don't like.
- ☐ I dislike running.

**Part C**

- ☐ I crave intense movement, such as sliding, swinging, and jumping.
- ☐ I like spinning, and I rarely get dizzy.
- ☐ I like the feel of unusual positions, such as head upside-down.
- ☐ I like to climb.
- ☐ I like to rock and twirl.
- ☐ I like to seek thrills through movement, such as going on rides at the fair.
- ☐ When I was younger, I used to move my head a lot (e.g., rocking, wagging, shaking).
- ☐ I like to crash into things, such as mattresses and pillows.
- ☐ People tell me I'm too boisterous. But really, I'm just trying to feel everything.

If you checked off more than 2 items in **Part A**, then you probably have some kind of difficulty with your gravity sense.

If you checked off more than 5 items in **Part B**, then you are probably **over-sensitive** in your gravity sense.

If you checked off more than 5 items in **Part C**, then you are probably **under-sensitive** in your gravity sense.

## Did you know?

*Without the tiny balance mechanisms in the inner ear, human beings would not be able to stand upright. You wouldm't know when your body was aligned with gravity, and you would fall over.*

# Gravity Sense Team Practice

A gravity sense team practice can help strengthen the nerve networks to your inner ear. The same activities help both over-sensitive and under-sensitive senses because they get your senses to communicate better.

The key idea in gravity sense team practice is **movement through space.**

## What Gravity Team Practices Can Do for You

- make you feel safer as you are doing your daily tasks
- make you better co-ordinated
- help you feel calm and steady inside
- help you feel relaxed in class so that you can listen and pay attention
- teach your brain-body to listen to messages about balance and movement
- reduce your anxiety
- stop grouchy moods and crazy moods

## Team Practice

Here are some suggestions for activities for a **weekly gravity team practice**. Choose **3 items** from this list. Your goal is to do each one **once a week** for **30 minutes**. If you have a special favorite, you might want to do the same activity three times a week. Choose activities that you like and feel most comfortable with first, and leave those that make you nervous until you feel more stable. These are your main team practices for the week.

**Dancing:** *Crank up the music and dance around your room. This gives your gravity sense a workout. Use as many different moves and positions as you can think of. A half-hour dance session will leave your gravity sense alert and fit.*

**Martial Arts:** *Martial arts use controlled movements to teach the body balance. A weekly karate class will help your gravity sense to co-ordinate with your other senses.*

**Swimming:** *Swimming allows you to move up, down, and around without dealing with gravity. Diving is especially helpful, since it turns your body (and your inner ear) upside down.*

**Rock-Climbing:** *Rock-climbing stimulates your gravity sense in an up-and-down direction. You can do this activity safely at a rock-climbing gym because safety straps will keep you from falling.*

**Trampoline:** *Trampoline activities allow your gravity sense to experience movement through space in many directions. Always work with an instructor or spotter in a well-supervised area.*

**Horseback Riding:** *You use many muscles and senses to keep yourself upright on a horse. The movement of the horse makes your gravity sense work to maintain your balance.*

**Cycling:** *You may not have liked cycling much as a kid because it took so long to learn. But now that you know how to cycle, keep it up. Your gravity sense gets a real workout on a bicycle. Consider cycling to school, to a friend's house, or to the store or library. Practice turning corners smoothly by leaning into the curve.*

**Fitness Ball Chair:** *Replace your chair with a fitness ball for doing homework or using the computer. The fitness ball forces your gravity sense to stay awake and work steadily and evenly throughout the day. A towel around the bottom will prevent it from rolling away.*

**Belly-Boarding:** *Buy a scooter board for rolling under cars. Surf around on a flat surface (such as an empty hallway, a gym, an uncarpeted basement, or a clean garage). Lie on your stomach and push off from the walls, as if you were swimming. Turn at walls and change directions. Wear garden gloves or hold nerf balls to prevent hurting your hands. Leave some objects scattered around the room to pick up as you go by.*

**Canoeing and Kayaking:** *If you tend to feel unsteady, then the unsteadiness of a canoe or kayak may seem overwhelming at first. Find a good instructor, go out on very calm days, and wear your life jacket all the time. Over time, you will feel more calm and in control.*

**Waterslide and Wave Pool:** *Waterslides and wave pools are great for feeling lifts, swings, and the pull of gravity.*

## Daily Warm-up Activities

Here are some suggestions for activities to use as daily team warm-ups. Choose an activity from this list to do every day for about **10 minutes.** Do a different one every day to discover which ones work best. Later, increase these activities to keep your gravity sense feeling alert and calm.

**Book Balance:** *This is an old-fashioned posture exercise. Place a heavy hardcover book on your head and walk around the room and up and down stairs. This exercise alerts all your senses to the correct position for perfect balance, so it's good for a morning warm-up.*

**Floor Activities:** *Crawl around on the floor on your hands and knees. Roll around on the floor. Do somersaults and cartwheels. Crawl up and down stairs. Get someone to hold your legs at the knees while you walk on your hands (the "wheelbarrow"). Floor activities let your gravity sense learn about different positions.*

**Rocking and Swinging:** *Swing in a swing or hammock or rock in a rocking chair. The back-and-forth motion keeps your gravity sense aware of changing positions. Try altering your position on a swing: standing, sitting, sitting sideways, and head down. Try rocking in a rocking chair with your head below and your feet up.*

**Diving:** *Whenever you go swimming, spend some time diving into deep water. Diving reverses your head position and gives your gravity sense a workout. If you can't dive yet, then swim underwater and try to get down to the bottom. Jump off the high board to give your gravity sense a deep up-and-down experience.*

**Fitness Ball Exercises:** *Use a fitness ball to do movement exercises, such as abdominal sit-ups or reverse sit-ups. Or just bounce around on it. In addition to strengthening your gravity sense, it will strengthen your abdomen and thighs.*

**Free-Falling:** *Stand at the edge of a thick foam mattress or a long, wide cushion or beanbag. Let yourself fall into it. Fall forward or backward. Do this several times to feel the movement through space and the satisfying crash at the end.*

## One-Minute Practice Ideas

Here are some suggestions for one-minute practices. Use these quickie activities when you need to increase your alertness right away. Feeling sluggish, bored, or fidgety are signs that your gravity sense needs stimulation right away.

**Head Turns:** *Gently and slowly tilt your head in a circle. Feel a light stretch in your neck. If you feel dizzy, slow it down.*

**Side Bends:** *Gently and slowly bend at the waist to your left side, then to your right side. Come back up slowly.*

**Jumps:** *Do a half-dozen small jumps on the spot. Or hop lightly from one foot to the other. Jumping jacks are another option.*

**Tiptoes:** *Go up on your tiptoes and down again several times.*

**Tipping on Your Chair:** *As long as your teacher is okay with this idea, tip your chair slightly backward, then back down again.*

**Squats:** *From a standing position, bend your knees till you are sitting on your heels, then stand up again.*

# Notes

# Review Gravity Sense

- The gravity sense is the brain-body's **awareness of the pull of gravity on the body**.
- If it is **over-sensitive**, you feel gravity too much and try to protect yourself from movement. If it is **under-sensitive**, you don't feel gravity enough and crave movement.
- The key idea of gravity team practice is **movement through space**. Gravity activities have lots of up-and-down and side-to-side movements. They help strengthen your gravity nerve networks.
- A regular gravity team practice will make you feel safer, more relaxed, and more in control of your moods.

## Gravity Activity Ideas That Interest Me

| WEEKLY | DAILY | ONE-MINUTE |
|---|---|---|
| ____ dancing | ____ book balance | ____ head turns |
| ____ martial arts | ____ floor activities | ____ side bends |
| ____ swimming | ____ rocking/swinging | ____ jumps |
| ____ rock-climbing | ____ diving | ____ tiptoes |
| ____ trampoline | ____ ball exercises | ____ tipping chair |
| ____ horseback riding | ____ free-falling | ____ squats |
| ____ cycling | ____________ | ____________ |
| ____ fitness ball chair | ____________ | ____________ |
| ____ belly-boarding | ____________ | ____________ |
| ____ canoeing/kayaking | ____________ | ____________ |
| ____ waterslide/wave pool | ____________ | ____________ |

## Questions to Consider

**1. I tried a few of these activities. But some of them made me feel sick. Should I stop?**

Yes. Always listen to your body. If an activity feels like too much, just go easy. But try again tomorrow and the next day. After a few days, your nerve networks will be stronger, and you'll get used to the sensations.

Other answers:

**2. Why do I feel embarrassed when I'm doing activities—even when I'm doing them alone?**

What you might be feeling is your brain-body's confusion. If your body is doing something new and awkward, it might send signals to the brain that the activity is embarrassing—even if there's nobody there to see you! If you can, try to ignore these feelings. Concentrate on the activity so that your brain is busy thinking about what you're doing.

Other answers:

**3. I am nervous about joining an activity class. I don't want the instructor thinking I'm a geek. That will make me feel really embarrassed.**

If you can get up the nerve, talk to the instructor privately before the class begins. Explain that you have a condition in your sense of balance. You don't have to explain much more than that. Ask for extra assistance. Let the instructor know you are hoping this activity will help improve things.

Other answers:

____________________________________________

____________________________________________

____________________________________________

**4. People will think I'm unco-ordinated if I join group activities.**

Many young people feel nervous when they start a new activity. If it is a class for beginners, then everyone is a beginner. Look at this as an opportunity to make friends with another nervous-looking person. You can even tell your new friend that you're not very co-ordinated and joke about it. People can be very understanding, especially when you are friendly.

Other answers:

____________________________________________

____________________________________________

____________________________________________

# Notes

# 4
# YOUR MUSCLE SENSE

Your **muscle sense** is your other movement sense. Your muscle sense is your brain-body's awareness of all your **muscles and joints**. The sensors are located in your muscles, joints, ligaments, and tendons. They feel two things: **movement and force**. The muscle sense works very closely with the gravity sense to help you move.

When the muscle sense is a strong player on your body-brain team, then your brain

- knows where all your body parts are, even when they are not moving
- knows how toned and action-ready each muscle is
- knows how long and heavy each body part is
- can guess the weight of an object before you pick it up

Your muscle sense sends many messages to the brain. When the muscle sense forgets to send even one message, the brain doesn't know what's going on. This leads to mistakes—missing, falling, tripping, dropping things, and bumping into things.

# BASES ARE LOADED

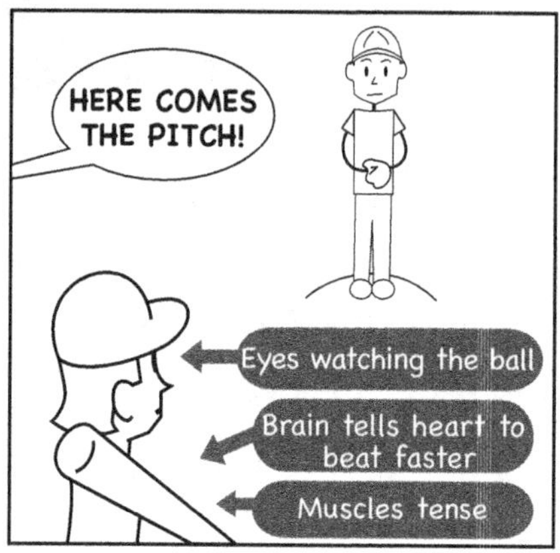

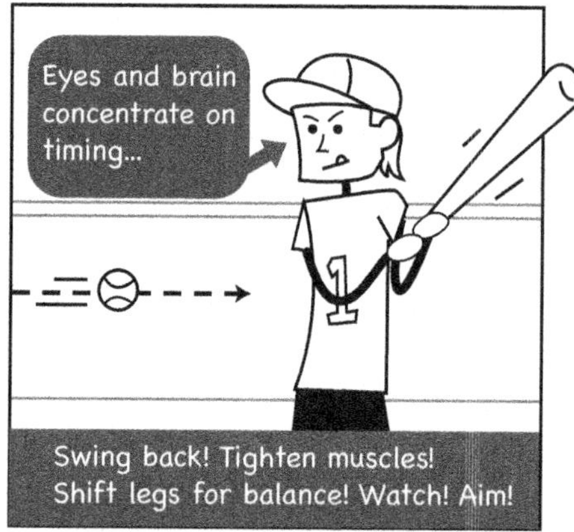

## Over-sensitivity and Under-sensitivity

Your muscle sense needs to be a strong, integrated player on your brain-body team. Sometimes it's over-sensitive or under-sensitive.

**Over-sensitive Muscle Sense:** The volume is **too high**. You feel muscle sensations too much, and this causes the brain to over-react. Your muscles end up uncoordinated. You tend to avoid movement to prevent these strong sensations.

**Under-sensitive Muscle Sense:** The volume is **too low**. You don't feel muscle sensation enough, sometimes not at all. Your brain-body makes you keep moving so that it can get information about where the muscles are, how toned they are, and whether they are ready to respond. You fidget and crave movement.

**Did you know?**

*You have more than 600 muscles in your body. Muscles make up about 40% of your weight.*

# Do you have difficulties with muscles?

**Part A**

- [ ] I don't play sports with much confidence because I often feel unco-ordinated.
- [ ] I don't like exercise. I prefer activities where I don't have to move around too much.
- [ ] I am not 100% right-handed or left-handed. I do some things with either hand.
- [ ] Actions on my left and right sides don't always match.
- [ ] When I stir things, some comes flying out of the bowl.
- [ ] My hands are not strong. I can't squeeze things well.

**Part B**

- [ ] I get tired easily in active sports.
- [ ] I hate doing aerobic classes because I can't follow the instructor. The moves are too complicated.
- [ ] I don't have a very good pencil/pen grip. My handwriting is untidy and hard to read. My hand gets tired quickly.
- [ ] I erase so hard I often rip the paper.
- [ ] I often break and drop things by accident.
- [ ] I snap pencil leads by accident.
- [ ] I am kind of bouncy. I can't sit still in a chair for very long.
- [ ] I'm not good at using screwdrivers and wrenches. It's hard to hold the tool and apply force at the same time.
- [ ] I liked being hugged hard. I seek out hugs because they feel good.
- [ ] Sometimes when I'm doing schoolwork, I have to lean my head on the desk.

**Part C**

- ☐ I dislike carrying heavy things.
- ☐ I dislike being in crowded rooms or hallways because I don't like being bumped by other people.
- ☐ I dislike hugs.
- ☐ I don't play racket sports well because I tend to hit the ball back too hard.
- ☐ People can get hurt playing with me because I use too much force without realizing it.
- ☐ I have posture problems. I tend to slump and slouch.
- ☐ My eyes sometimes go out of focus and I see double.
- ☐ If I have to lift two objects that don't weigh the same, I either lift one of them too hard or don't lift the other one enough.
- ☐ Sometimes my boots feel too heavy for my legs.

If you checked off more than 3 items in **Part A**, then you probably have muscle sense difficulties.

If you checked off more than 5 items in **Part B**, then you are probably **under-sensitive** in your muscle sense.

If you checked off more than 5 items in **Part C**, then you are probably **over-sensitive** in your muscle sense.

## Did you know?

*The tiny muscles around your eyes are about 100 times more powerful than they need to be—so that you can move your eyes fast.*

# Muscle Sense Team Practices

A muscle sense team practice can help strengthen the nerve networks to your muscles and joints. The same exercises help both over-sensitive and under-sensitive senses because they work by exercising the senses and getting them to communicate better with the brain-body.

The key idea in muscle team workout activities is **hard muscle work.**

There are several types of activities:

- activities that stimulate the left and right sides of your body to work together
- activities that crash, smash, or press the body, exercising your joints and tendons
- activities that make your muscles pull, push, or lift

## What a Muscle Sense Team Practice Can Do for You

- make you feel stronger and more confident
- make you more co-ordinated
- help you feel calm and steady inside
- help you feel relaxed in class so that you can listen and pay attention
- teach your brain-body to listen to your muscles and joints
- reduce your anxiety
- stop grouchy moods and crazy moods

## Team Practice

Here are some suggestions for activities for a weekly gravity team practice. Choose **3 items** from this list. Your goal is to do each one **once a week** for **30 minutes.** If you have a special favorite, you might want to do the same activity 3 times a week. Choose activities that you like and feel most comfortable with first, and leave those that make you nervous until you feel more stable. These are your main team practices for the week.

**Gravity Sense Activities:** *Many of the activities for the gravity sense work just as well for the muscle sense, since both senses work together to perform most sports and games. These activities involve pushing, pulling, hitting, crashing, bouncing, grabbing, and lifting, as well as moving through space.*

**Heavy Work:** *Your body likes the feel of muscles and joints being pressed and pulled. So hauling, pushing, pulling, lifting, kicking, hitting, and yanking feel good. Chopping wood and carrying boxes are great. If those aren't available, then consider getting a punching bag.*

**Strength Training:** *Visit your school's universal gym. Ask a teacher to show you how to use the weights and exercise machines. Do each activity for as many reps as the teacher suggests, rest, then do another set. At first, you will be able to lift or press only small weights. But keep it up. In three weeks, most beginners can lift three times the weight they started with.*

**Chores:** *Offer to do more chores around the house. You could negotiate an extra allowance at the same time, but the stunned look you get might be worth it all on its own! Remember that your body likes hard work, so after it gets over the initial sluggishness, it will enjoy doing these tasks.*

**Swimming Lessons:** *Swimming lessons teach you new swimming strokes. New activities give your muscle networks something new to communicate about. Ask your swimming instructor to help you co-ordinate your right and left sides.*

**Drumming:** *Take a drumming course. You don't need to buy an expensive drum kit: a small hand drum works fine. Some instructors prefer plastic garbage bins turned upside-down. Listen carefully so that you are aware when one hand is drumming harder than the other.*

**Walking and Hiking:** *Walk to school and home every day. If that is too far, then get off the bus two or three stops early and walk the rest of the way. Join a hiking club that goes for walks in woodlands on weekends. Walking over uneven ground and up and down hills makes your muscles work hard and squeezes your joints.*

**Carpentry:** *Use a hammer and nails to build things. Work with an instructor who can teach you about safety and can take the time to help you steady your hands. While your first project might not be very impressive, your second and third ones will be much better. In the meantime, you will have strengthened your arm muscles and given them a pounding workout.*

## Daily Warm-up Activity Ideas

Here are some suggestions for activities to use as daily warm-ups. Choose an activity from this list to do every day for about **10 minutes.** Do a different one every day till you discover which ones seem to work best. Later, increase these activities to keep your muscle sense feeling alert and calm.

**Stairs:** *Take the stairs whenever you can, rather than escalators and elevators.*

**Weight Belts:** *Buy a weightlifter's support belt at a fitness store. Wear it for short periods while at home. The compression will feel good.*

**Jump Rope:** *Leave a skipping rope near the back door. Before you walk to school, do 20 quick skips.*

**Resistance Bands:** *Buy a stretchy resistance band at a home healthcare store or fitness store. Do two or three of the exercises in the instruction booklet every day.*

**Wrestling:** *Find a willing parent or sibling to wrestle with. Arm wrestling is good too. The goal is not to "win" but to experience the press and pull of your muscles. Try making a "people sandwich" with two other people. Or have a regular pillow fight that includes pressing and crushing.*

**Ankle Weights:** *Attach a 2 or 5 lb (1 or 2.5 kg) weight-band to your ankles while you are at home. Walk around the house and do your usual activities. The added weight forces you to move more carefully and gives your leg muscles a lot of sensory input. Remove them after 10 minutes so that you don't strain your leg muscles.*

**Vibration:** *Vibration shakes the muscles and joints, which gives the brain-body a lot of soothing information. Deep pressure vibrators are best, but they are often hard to find. An alternative is to sit on the clothes dryer when it's running.*

**Backpacks:** *Carry a backpack to school every day. Don't load it down: keep the weight comfortable on your back but firm on your shoulders. Make sure the backpack has two shoulder straps, so that the weight is equal on both sides. Backpacks exercise back and leg muscles from the shoulders to your feet.*

**Walk 'n Stretch:** *If you walk past a playground on your way to school, take a minute to hang on the climber. If you can, walk your hands along the climber till the end. This will stretch your upper body and wake up your arm muscles.*

**Evening Run:** *An evening run doesn't have to be far, and it doesn't have to be fast. To start, run barely faster than you walk. Ten minutes on your feet in the fresh air will leave you feeling refreshed and awake.*

## One-Minute Practice Ideas

Here are some suggestions for one-minute practices. Use these quickie activities when you need to increase or decrease your alertness. Feeling sleepy, irritable, or fidgety are signs that your muscle sense may need stimulation right away.

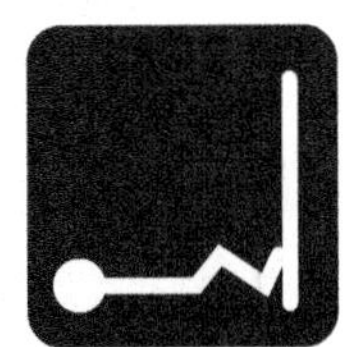

**Foot Presses:** *While lying down, push your feet against a wall. This wakes up the muscles along the length of your body.*

**Arm Lifts:** *Lift your arms to the ceiling, tilt your head back, and stretch. This wakens all your muscles and joints. If you are alone, yell at the same time.*

**Finger Stretches:** *To avoid breaking pencil leads (and to improve your handwriting), stretch your fingers before doing any writing activity. This wakes up the small finger muscles so that they use even pressure on the pencil and paper.*

**Hand Presses:** *Press your hands together hard so that your fingers are flat against each other. This wakes up your hand and arm muscles. It helps keep you from dropping things. You can also (quietly) crack your knuckles.*

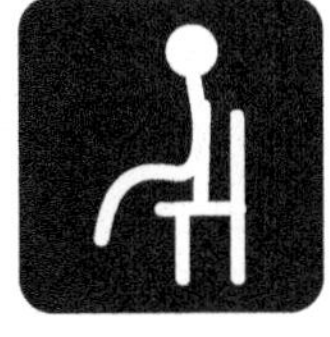

**Chair Push-ups:** *While sitting on a hard chair, grip the edges of the chair's seat on both sides and push yourself up off the chair. Hold yourself in the air for a few seconds, then release back down.*

**Classroom Tasks:** *Offer to wipe the chalkboard, stack the chairs, move the gym mats, or staple the handouts. This gives you a little break to get up and move during class.*

**Hand Fidgets:** *Some people can concentrate better in class if they have something to squeeze or play with in their hands. These little toys are called hand fidgets. Some are small balloons filled with sand, and others are squeeze balls.*

# Review Muscle Sense

- The muscle sense is your brain-body's awareness of all your **muscles, joints, and ligaments**—where they are, how they feel, and what they're doing.
- An **over-sensitive** muscle sense feels muscle sensations too much and causes the brain to over-react. An **under-sensitive** muscle sense doesn't feel muscle sensation enough and causes the brain to crave movement.
- The key idea in muscle team practices is **heavy work**. This helps strengthen your muscle nerve networks.
- A regular muscle team practice will help you feel calm, confident, relaxed, and in control. It will also help you control your moods.

## Muscle Activity Ideas That Interest Me

**WEEKLY**

____ gravity activities
____ heavy work
____ strength training
____ chores
____ swimming lessons
____ drumming
____ walking and hiking
____ carpentry
__________________
__________________

**DAILY**

____ stairs
____ weight belts
____ jump rope
____ resistance bands
____ wrestling
____ ankle weights
____ vibration
____ backpacks
____ walk 'n stretch
____ evening run

**ONE-MINUTE**

____ foot presses
____ arm lifts
____ finger stretches
____ hand presses
____ chair push-ups
____ classroom tasks
____ hand fidgets
__________________
__________________
__________________

## Questions to Consider

**1. Why do my muscles hurt when I do heavy work, like shovelling or lifting?**

Your muscles might not be strong enough yet for the tasks you are trying to do. If they hurt, then the muscles might be sending a signal to the brain that they can't handle it. Your muscles might also be over-sensitive to the feeling of hard work. Start small. Go with the smallest or lightest task you can, then work your way up slowly over several days.

Other answers:

________________________________________

________________________________________

________________________________________

**2. Why do my muscles feel wobbly when I do heavy work?**

Because they are working very hard but aren't quite strong enough. Let them rest for a day, then try again. When they feel wobbly again, stop and let them rest. You can also reduce the amount of heavy work you are doing so that the muscles don't have to work so hard.

Other answers:

________________________________________

________________________________________

________________________________________

# Notes

# Notes

# 5
# YOUR SENSE OF TOUCH

Your sense of touch (sometimes called the *tactile sense*) is your awareness of the feelings of your skin. The sensors are located in your skin all over your body. These skin sensors feel **temperature** (hot, cold), **texture** (rough, smooth, bumpy, slippery, sharp), and **pain** (a little or a lot).

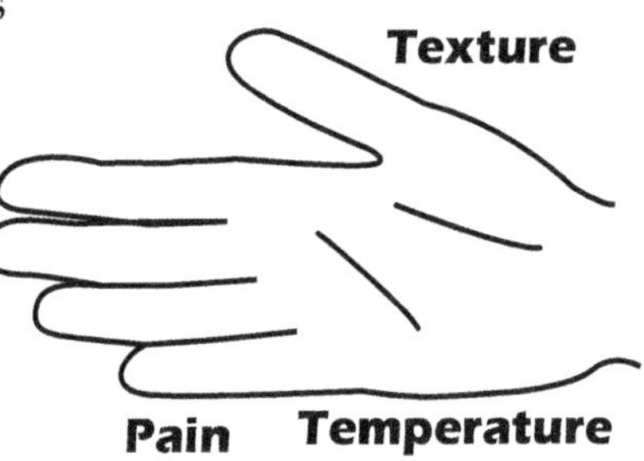


When the sense of touch is a strong, integrated player on the brain-body team

- it sends messages to the brain quickly and efficiently
- it knows instantly when a mosquito has landed on your arm (so that you have time to slap it)
- it feels pain and reacts to it with the right amount of alarm
- it adapts quickly to changes, such as the warmth of a shower, the cool sensation of rain, the feel of a new shirt, or the texture of a new food in your mouth
- it allows you to enjoy sensations, such as the feel of clay in art class, hugs from a parent, and someone brushing your hair

The sense of touch often works together with the muscle sense and the gravity sense to give your brain-body information about situations. If these senses are not communicating well, then you will have a hard time figuring out your world. You will hurt yourself often and feel afraid a lot of the time.

## Danger and Exploration

The sense of touch does **two important jobs** for the brain-body:

### Job #1. Danger Protection

Your sense of touch alerts your brain-body about danger and gets you to move out of harm's way. This is a strong, fast message, and your body reacts to it instantly.

### Job #2. Exploration

Your sense of touch allows you to explore things and learn about them. It lets you enjoy the feel of things. It also helps you figure out what something is without looking at it.

# RISE AND SHINE

Both jobs are important. When one job crowds out the other, there are problems. If your sense of touch is too focused on danger protection, you will sense every touch sensation as danger and will become a sensation avoider. If it is too explorative, your sense of touch will crave more sensation, and you will become a sensation seeker—even when sensations are dangerous.

- If your sense of touch is too high on danger protection, then it is **over-sensitive**. You feel touch sensations too strongly. Everything feels too rough, too hot, too cold, too slippery, too soggy, or too wet.
- If it is too high on exploration, then it is **under-sensitive**. You don't feel when things are happening. You might not realize when you are being touched. You might not be aware that your face is dirty or your belt is twisted.

## Is your sense of touch over-sensitive or under-sensitive?

**Part A**

- ☐ I don't like the feel of eating with my fingers.
- ☐ I hate being touched lightly. It makes my skin crawl or it feels too ticklish. I always want to rub it away.
- ☐ I avoid situations where I might get touched a lot accidentally, such as crowded hallways.
- ☐ Cuts and bruises seem to hurt me more than they hurt others. People tell me I over-react about little things.

- [ ] I always cut the tags out of my shirts.
- [ ] I like soft clothes that have been washed a lot. I don't like new clothes. I prefer waistbands with elastic.
- [ ] When I was little, I hated baths, especially getting my hair washed. I didn't like the feel of water on my face. Sometimes I still hate it.
- [ ] I don't like to eat food when it's hot.
- [ ] I feel cold weather more than other people do.
- [ ] I don't like windy days.
- [ ] I don't like the feel of a toothbrush. I dislike going to the dentist.

**Part B**

- [ ] I tend to touch people a lot, more than they like.
- [ ] I often have food on my face or hands and can't feel it.
- [ ] I like petting cats and dogs for a long time.
- [ ] I used to have certain toys that I played with because I liked the feel of them.
- [ ] I often get cuts or bruises without feeling them. Even when I was little, I never cried when I got cuts because I hardly noticed them.
- [ ] I sometimes put my shirt on backwards.
- [ ] Sometimes when I'm carrying several things, I drop some of them and don't notice that I've dropped them.
- [ ] I often don't notice if a room is hot or cold.
- [ ] I sometimes chew on my pencil, my fingernails, or my shirt sleeves.
- [ ] I bump into people a lot without realizing it.

If you checked off more than 5 items in **Part A**, then your sense of touch is probably **over-sensitive** and too strong on **danger protection**.

If you checked off more than 5 items in **Part B**, then your sense of touch is probably **under-sensitive** and too strong on **exploration**.

# Touch Sense Team Practices

To bring your sense of touch into the comfortable zone between over-sensitive and under-sensitive, you need to get it familiar and comfortable with lots of sensations.

Touch team practices can help even out your sense of touch. The key idea in touch team workout activities is **variety of touch**.

## What a Touch Team Practice Can Do for You

- make you less sensitive and fearful of touch, texture, temperature, and pain
- make you more aware of touch sensations
- get you accustomed to many different sensations
- help you feel relaxed in class so that you can listen and pay attention
- reduce your anxiety

## Team Practice and Warm-Up Activity Ideas

Here are some suggestions for activities for daily and weekly touch sense team practices. Choose various items from this list to do **daily** for **10–30 minutes** each. Choose activities that you like and feel most comfortable with first, and leave those that make you nervous until you feel more relaxed.

**Random Stimulation:** *Choose a selection of textures (sponges, facecloths, soft brushes, loofahs) and lightly rub them against your skin for a few minutes. If you find you hate the sensation, try doing it more lightly or more firmly.*

**Foot Rollers:** *Many bath shops sell wooden foot massagers that you roll under your bare feet. These feel weird at first. As you get used to the new sensation, you'll find it feels good.*

**Groping in the Dark:** *When you are looking for something, try doing it with your hands, rather than your eyes. When you know something is buried at the bottom of your backpack or purse, try groping and feeling for it without looking. Make a point of trying to identify things by how they feel.*

**Random Showers:** *If you have a showerhead that has different sprays, try a new setting every time you have a shower. Experiment with shower temperatures too. Start with a comfortable temperature, then adjust it very slightly warmer. When you feel okay with it, change it again.*

**Art Classes:** *Sign up for an art class. Try to concentrate on being creative so that you don't focus too much on your messy hands. If you can't tolerate doing art with your hands, then choose a tool that allows you to keep your hands clean, or wear gloves. Concentrate on feeling the pressure and the sensations of this tool as your hand moves it.*

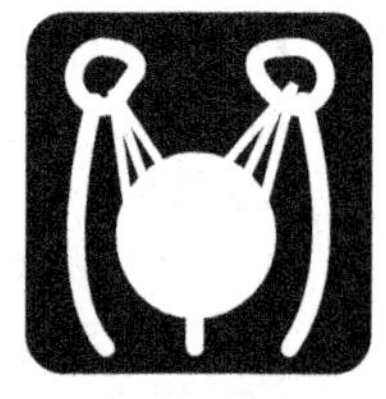

**Hair Tugs:** *Tug at your hair. Don't yank out handfuls, just give gentle tugs. It might feel a bit odd, but should not be alarming. This activity alerts the skin sensors in your scalp. You'll find it easier to wash your hair, comb your hair, and get haircuts.*

**Music Class:** *Learn to play a musical instrument, such as in band class. Playing an instrument involves lots of touch sensations, such as feeling the holes of the instrument with your fingertips and moving your fingers in time with the conductor.*

**Cooking:** *Cooking allows you to explore the feel of foods. Don't be afraid to touch a fruit or vegetable before you chop it, or to scoop your hands through rice or dried beans. If the texture bothers you too much, consider wearing latex gloves. You will still be able to feel the squish, weight, and texture of the food you are working with.*

## Accommodations

Some people with an over-sensitive sense of touch need more than activities and practices. They also need to get rid of annoying sensations.

The following suggestions are for **accommodations**—changes you make to your world so that you don't have to put up with irritating sensations. Reducing irritation will help your skin feel calm throughout the day.

**Soft Clothes:** *Get involved in choosing your clothes. You might prefer to wear pre-washed or used clothing. You might like natural cotton more than artificial fabrics, or elastic waists more than zipper-and-belt waists. Discover what feels comfortable and buy those clothes.*

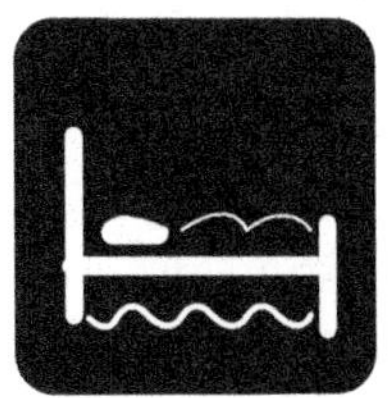

**Soft Bedding:** *Help choose your bedding. High-quality cotton sheets are smoother than regular sheets. Choose a bedspread or quilt with just the right weight to feel comfortable. Arrange to have layers of bedding so that you can choose exactly how much weight and warmth you want every night. Getting a good night's sleep will help you cope with whatever happens during the day.*

**Evening Shower or Bath:** *An evening shower or bath that is exactly the right temperature and exactly the right length will help you relax for sleep. Dry off with a super-soft, high-quality towel.*

# Notes

# Review Sense of Touch

- The sense of touch is your awareness of the **sensations of your skin**—such as **texture**, **pain**, and **temperature**.
- The sense of touch has two jobs: (1) to protect you from **danger**, and (2) to allow you to **explore** things.
- An **over-sensitive** touch sense is too high on danger protection. An **under-sensitive** touch sense is too high on exploration.
- The key idea of a touch sense team practice is a **variety of touch sensations**. This helps strengthen your touch nerve networks.
- Regular touch team practices will help you feel less anxious and worried. You will be better able to cope with new sensations.

## Touch Ideas That Interest Me

**ACTIVITIES**

____ random stimulation

____ random showers

____ groping in the dark

____ foot rollers

____ art classes

____ hair tugs

____ music class

____ cooking

**ACCOMMODATIONS**

____ soft clothes

____ soft bedding

____ evening shower or bath

______________________

______________________

______________________

______________________

______________________

## Questions to Consider

**1. I want to look good, but I don't like the feel of most clothes.**

Buy clothes at used clothing stores. They have already been washed, shrunk, and softened. You can develop your own style by avoiding the tight, uncomfortable clothes that are in style that year and choosing older clothes in great colors.

Other answers:

______________________________________________

______________________________________________

______________________________________________

**2. Why do "touchy" activities sometimes makes me feel weird?**

That feeling is caused by *adrenaline,* an alarm chemical in your body. It tells your body that a situation is dangerous. But adrenaline also makes your senses feel things more strongly. So the more "weird" you feel, the more strongly you will feel those "touchy" activities. Wait a few minutes to let the adrenaline go down before trying again.

Other answers:

______________________________________________

______________________________________________

**3. Why does rubbing brushes and things against my skin make me feel good? Shouldn't it make me feel bad?**

Brushing and rubbing different textures against your skin exercises your skin sensors. They wake up and become very alert. That alert feeling passes through your whole body. When your body is alert, your brain-body feels calm and safe.

Other answers:

______________________________________________

______________________________________________

______________________________________________

# Notes

# 6
# YOUR MOUTH SENSES

The **mouth senses** are all the senses that are connected to your mouth.

The main mouth senses are

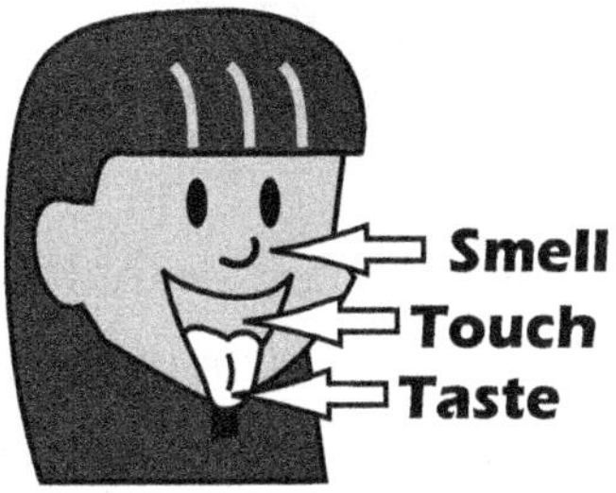

- **taste** (located in the taste-buds of your tongue and throat)
- **touch** (located in the skin of your lips and mouth)
- **smell** (located in the nose, above the mouth)



These three senses control your **reaction to food**. When they are strong players on your mouth team, then

- you enjoy eating
- you like new tastes and textures
- you quickly identify tastes that are harmful

But when these senses are not strong players on your mouth team, then food is always irritating, alarming, and even nauseating. Meals might be unbearable.

**Did you know?**

*Humans have about 9,000 taste-buds on their tongue. Pigs have 15,000, and rabbits have 17,000.*

## Your Mouth Sense of Taste

The taste sense has **two main jobs:**

**Job #1. Danger Protection:** Certain tastes mean danger, such as poison, mold, or bacteria. If you bite something rotten, your taste-buds should react immediately and make you spit it out. Young children have extra taste-buds in their throat, so that if they taste something bitter (the most common taste of poisons), they will automatically gag and spit.

**Job #2. Exploration:** Most tastes are enjoyable. After all, nature wants humans to eat. So taste helps us identify foods that are enjoyable and nutritious. Before the invention of artificial flavors, good taste meant good nutrition.

A sense of taste that is too high in danger protection is **over-sensitive**. If you avoid food that's even a little bit spicy, salty, or strong-tasting, then you are probably over-sensitive. Your taste-buds over-react to strong-tasting food because it seems dangerous.

A sense of taste that is too high in exploration is **under-sensitive**. If you crave strong flavors and don't care if food is burnt, going bad, stale, or weird-tasting, then your mouth senses are probably under-sensitive.

# ON TODAY'S MENU

THE FOODS I **HATE**? HMM... THAT WOULD BE COOKED MUSHY VEGETABLES, MUSHY FRUIT. OKAY... ANYTHING **COOKED AND MUSHY**...

... AND **HOT, SPICY FOODS**, LIKE CHILI. AND COLD LUMPY FOODS LIKE TAPIOCA PUDDING. AND SLIMY FOODS, AND SOUR FOODS...

... LASAGNA, SALADS WITH DRESSING, ANY KIND OF FISH, ANYTHING WITH **PEPPER OR LEMON OR BARBEQUE SAUCE**, ANY KIND OF SHARP CHEESE...

... MEAT THAT IS HARD TO CHEW, MEATS COVERED IN GRAVIES AND SAUCES, FOODS THAT ARE **MIXED TOGETHER**...

FOODS THAT I **LIKE**? WELL, UM...

... ANYTHING **PLAIN AND DRY**, PREFERABLY **WHITE**. THAT'S MY SPECIALTY!

### Childhood Taste-Buds

Young children have more taste-buds than teens and adults. This helps protect children from poisoning. Children have extra taste-buds at the top of their throat that make them throw up if they eat strong-tasting or weird-tasting food. You might remember gagging on certain foods when you were little.

These gagging taste-buds start to disappear when you are about 12 years old. So if you disliked many foods as a young child and have avoided them ever since, now might be the time to give them a second chance. You might be surprised to find they become your favorites now.

## Your Mouth Sense of Touch

The skin inside your mouth gives you information about the **texture** of food—whether it is **smooth**, **lumpy**, **crunchy**, or **soft**. Some people hate the feel of certain food textures. Other people are okay with different food textures as long as they are separate. For example, you might like bread, cheese, and tomato sauce but hate pizza. The combination of these textures (and tastes) feels disturbing in your mouth.

Some people are the opposite: they can't really feel the food at all. Their lips, cheeks, and gums barely feel the sensation of the food. This can end up making food very messy, since it can start slipping out of their mouth without their even knowing it!

## Your Mouth Sense of Smell

**Smell** is another part of the food experience. We tend to smell food the way we taste it. Some of the smell of a food passes through the top of the mouth into the nose. You might notice that when you have a cold with a blocked nose, you can't taste food very well.

Smell might not be the most important sense to humans, but it still has power over our brain-bodies. Smells can trigger good moods and bad moods. Some people believe that smells go even deeper than that. For example, people who do **aromatherapy** believe that smells can help cure illnesses and disorders. Certainly smells can influence our moods. Deep breathing of clean, fresh air often makes us feel more calm and happy.

### Did you know?

*Dogs can distinguish the smell of T-shirts of identical twins. Babies can recognize the smell of their mother.*

## What are your food preferences?

- ☐ I like food to be strong-tasting. I use lots of ketchup, salt, pepper, hot sauce, pepperoni, and other spices. I really like sour candies.
- ☐ I like white foods like noodles, bread, potatoes (fries), cereal, and milk.
- ☐ I like to keep my foods separate on my plate. I don't like mixed foods.
- ☐ I don't like cooked vegetables because they become mushy. I will eat them raw when they are crunchy.
- ☐ When I eat spaghetti, I prefer to eat the noodles separate from the sauce.
- ☐ I don't really taste food very much. I can eat pretty much anything as long as I can add some salt to it.
- ☐ I eat each thing on my plate one at a time until it is finished. I don't like mixing the tastes.
- ☐ I like putting weird things together, like ketchup on bread, or pickles with peanut butter.
- ☐ I notice weird food smells as soon as I enter a room. I have to block my nose till I get used to it.
- ☐ I like to smell foods. I often smell everything on my plate before I start eating.

## Other Mouth Senses

The mouth includes the two movement senses as well. The **muscle sense** and the **gravity sense** are connected to the mouth. **Chewing and crunching** work the muscles in the jaw, which belong to the muscle sense. Chewing and crunching also help the gravity sense, because your jawbone is located very close to your inner ear. So chewy and crunchy food can give several of your senses a workout.

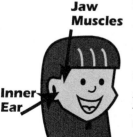

## Nutrition, Eating, and the Mouth Senses

The mouth senses are important because they control your **eating** and **nutrition**. Good nutrition—such as lots of fresh fruits, vegetables, and proteins—keeps all your senses healthy. Poor nutrition—such as junk food and too much white starchy food—starves the team and weakens it. If you avoid foods because your mouth senses are over-sensitive, or if you eat spicy junk food because your mouth senses are under-sensitive, you may end up starving yourself for nutrition, making the situation worse.

**Breakfast** is the most important meal of the day because it affects your **blood sugar**. Blood sugar is the food your blood carries through your body to give you energy. A breakfast that is too high in sugars and starches—such as sugary cereals or waffles with syrup—will spike your blood sugar levels. You'll feel bouncy and fidgety. Later in the morning, your blood sugar will get used up and will suddenly drop, and you will feel very tired and irritable.

To avoid sugar spikes and drops, eat low-sugar breakfast foods—such as fruit and whole-grain cereals—and include some protein—such as eggs, yogurt, peanut butter, or meat.

## Food Allergies and Intolerances

**Food allergies** are not the same as mouth sensitivities. If you have a food allergy, it's caused by your **immune system**, not your senses. A food allergy will make you sick. You may have a rash, dizziness, or nausea. A doctor can help you figure out if you have any food allergies.

A **food intolerance** is different from a food allergy. It's caused by your **digestive system**. Some people are **lactose intolerant**, which means they can't digest milk. Other people are **wheat intolerant** (or *celiac*), which means they can't digest wheat. Lactose intolerance and celiac disorders cause stomach pain, irritability, and tiredness. Anyone who is lactose intolerant or celiac without knowing it will have irritation all the time. This causes a lot of difficulties for their senses, especially if they are over-sensitive. If you are lactose or wheat intolerant, then getting rid of these irritations will make life a lot more comfortable.

**Did you know?**

*About 70% of the world's people are lactose intolerant. About 10% of North Americans are celiac, and most don't know it.*

## Mealtimes

Healthy **meals** are important for keeping your brain-body calm and alert. But if your mouth senses are sensation avoiders, then after a hard day at school you are going to find it hard to sit down to a plate of different kinds of foods. Your senses will be irritable and withdrawn.

Take time at the end of the school day to do activities to soothe and alert your senses. Keep moving. Then you will go to your dinner plate feeling fresh and relaxed. It may end up not looking so bad. It will probably taste and feel good too.

## Eating Habits

**Habits** are another part of eating, because what you eat is connected to your emotions and experiences. If people have had bad experiences with a food in the past, they will avoid it, sometimes forever. Avoidance is a habit, and habits are hard to break. Some people believe that their tastes will never change. But tastes do change, and so do people.

If you have had over-sensitive taste-buds all your life, then you may have become accustomed to experiencing foods as **objects of danger**. Danger messages might have become routine every time you look at a new food. Think about those danger messages. Are these foods really dangerous? Do other people find them dangerous? By expecting a bad experience, are you making a bad experience happen? Since your taste-buds have changed since your early childhood, your experience now probably won't be as intense as in the past.

Food is **social**, so missing out on food is missing out on fun. It will be easier to be out with friends if you can eat more of the foods they eat. Food can be a lot of fun, too, so don't let old habits and memories get in the way.

**Did you know?**

*Fresh carrots, tomatoes, and celery contain more water than whole milk. That is because plants hold water in all their cells. Meanwhile, whole milk contains a lot of protein and fat.*

# Mouth Senses Team Practice

Mouth team practices are useful because the mouth senses are like a shortcut to all the senses in the brain-body. When you are short on time or need a quick team wake-up, try a mouth activity.

## What a Mouth Team Practice Can Do for You

- make you less sensitive and fearful about new tastes
- make you feel calm and alert
- help you enjoy a wider variety of foods
- improve your nutrition and help you like more foods
- reduce your anxiety about eating other people's food
- help you relax in class so you can listen and pay attention
- help you identify foods and food sensations that make you feel good
- help get you out of a grouchy mood or stop a crazy mood

## Team Practices

**Eat Nutritious Food:** *Think about the food you eat. Make sure you are getting enough protein, fruits, and vegetables. Eat different cold, hot, chewy, crunchy, and wet foods every day.*

**Try Aromatherapy:** *If you like smells, you might find aromatherapy useful. Aromatherapy uses bottled scents that have been shown to affect people's emotions. Many health stores carry aromatherapy products. They may help keep you alert to do homework or soothe you as you get ready for bed.*

## Strategies for Trying New Foods

Trying new foods? If you say *yuck*, then you've probably had a difficult time with food tastes and textures over the years. But the teen and pre-teen years are a good time to try them again. Take it slowly, and you may find you like a lot more than you thought you did.

Here are some suggestions to help you get used to new foods.

**Examine Your Fears:** *Why do you dislike foods? Is it because of the taste, texture, or smell? Is it because you were forced to eat it when you were little, so that now it makes you gag even before you taste it? Is it habit? Is your danger protection response over-reacting? Once you know the reason, then you can develop a strategy for tackling it.*

**Start Small:** *What is the smallest amount of the new food that you could eat? This could be a serving as small as one pea, one slice of a grape, or one teaspoon of juice. Start by just touching it and looking at it. Then just touch it to your lips. Set your goal to work up to eating a tiny piece every day till you get used to it. Let your taste-buds learn that there is no danger.*

**Learn to Cook:** *Ask a parent to help you learn to cook. Have "your day" to make supper or lunch. Start with meals that involve very little cooking, such as raw vegetables, fruit, toast, and cold meats. When you feel ready, try learning to boil macaroni, microwave frozen vegetables, or bake oven fries.*

## One-Minute Practices — The Mouth Tools

Because so many senses are attached to the mouth, you can use mouth activities to keep all your senses feeling good. You can think of these mouth activities as **mouth tools**.

Mouth tools are very handy, because they work fast, and you can carry some with you in your pocket or backpack. They are especially good for helping you get control of your mood.

Experiment with these mouth tools to discover which ones work best for you. Then keep some handy. Ask your teacher if you can keep some (e.g., a spout water-bottle or gum) at your desk.

**Cold Food** *(ice cream, yogurt, popsicles):*

- *wakes you up when you are sleepy*
- *stimulates the brain to think*
- *helps get you out of a grouchy mood*

**Warm Food** *(tea, freshly baked bread, pizza, hot chocolate):*

- *soothes your emotions*
- *helps stop a crazy mood*

**Sweet Food** *(candy, cookies, honey):*

- *soothes your senses*
- *gives you energy if you are falling asleep*

**Sour Food** *(sour candies, sweet-and-sour sauce):*

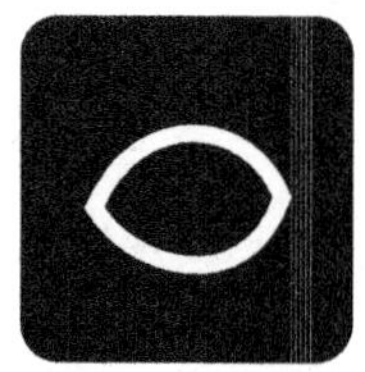

- *wakes you up*
- *wakes up your senses*

**Chewy Food** *(gum, licorice, caramels, gummy bears, jerky, dried fruit):*

- *helps you remember and learn*
- *helps keep your focus*
- *helps prevent queasiness and motion sickness*
- *helps you relax*
- *helps get you out of a grouchy mood or stop a crazy mood*

**Crunchy Food** *(crisp fruit and vegetables, granola bars, cereals, cookies, nuts, popcorn):*

- *wakes you up if you are sleepy*
- *keeps your brain alert*
- *provides stimulation to your muscle sense that might allow you to sit still longer*
- *helps get you out of a grouchy mood or stop a crazy mood*

**Carbonated Drinks** *(soda pop, cider):*

- *helps stimulate your alertness*
- *soothes by providing interesting mouth stimulation*
- *helps get you out of a grouchy mood or stop a crazy mood*

**Sucking Food** *(drinking through a straw, frozen chocolate chips, hard candy):*

- *soothes your emotions*
- *stimulates your brain to respond to the senses*
- *helps all senses feel calm and relaxed*
- *helps get you out of a grouchy mood or stop a crazy mood*

**Smelling Food** *(cinnamon sticks, vanilla, baking bread):*

- *soothes your emotions*
- *stimulates hunger*

**Blowing** *(blowing air through your mouth as if blowing out birthday candles, blowing bubbles):*

- *helps reduce tension and relax the body*

**Did you know?**

*The human mouth can taste four different tastes: bitter, sweet, sour, and salty. It is more sensitive to bitter tastes than to any of the others.*

# Notes

# Review Mouth Senses

- The mouth senses include **taste, touch, and smell**.
- They have two jobs: (1) **danger protection**, and (2) **exploration**. **Over-sensitive** mouth senses are too high in danger protection, and **under-sensitive** mouth senses are too high in exploration.
- The jaw muscles and inner ear are close to the mouth, so the **muscle and gravity senses** are involved in eating too.
- **Nutrition** is important for healthy nerve networks, so you need to learn to eat a variety of healthy foods.
- Foods that you disliked as a young child can easily become your favorites now, if you let yourself get used to them little by little.
- **Mouth tools** are the most important part of the mouth senses team practice. Learn which ones work for you.

## Mouth Activity Ideas That Interest Me

**ACTIVITIES**

____ eat nutritious food

____ try aromatherapy

**NEW FOODS**

____ examine fears

____ start small

____ learn to cook

**MOUTH TOOLS**

____ cold food

____ warm food

____ sweet food

____ sour food

____ chewy food

____ crunchy food

____ carbonated drink

____ sucking food

____ smelling food

____ blowing

______________________

## Questions to Consider

**1. I don't want to learn to cook. I'm afraid I might burn myself.**

Cooking doesn't need to involve heat. You can simply cut up raw or cold food. You can heat food in the microwave. You don't need to use the stove until you feel ready.

Other answers:

________________________________________

________________________________________

________________________________________

**2. Do I need to learn to use a knife and fork? I'm not good at it. I eat with my fingers.**

Finger muscles control your knife and fork. If your finger muscles aren't strong, then they might not have the control right now. You might find it helpful to do finger exercises before you try using a knife and fork, such as finger stretches and hand presses. This will help wake up the small hand muscles. Try holding the knife and fork firmly and using them in the middle of the plate.

Other answers:

________________________________________

________________________________________

________________________________________

**3. What if my school won't allow me to carry gum, water, or granola bars to class?**

You may need to get your parents to help you arrange special privileges in class. At the very least, the school should be able to allow you to carry a sports water-bottle with a spout so that you can suck on water when you are losing attention. Always make these special arrangements privately, not in front of other students.

Other answers:

______________________________________________

______________________________________________

______________________________________________

**4. I would like to lose weight. Will eating nutritious foods be like going on a diet?**

Losing weight is not the reason to eat nutritious food. The real reason is to keep your brain-body healthy. In every aspect of your life, you will feel better if you eat good, healthy food. Nutritious food is not a weight-loss diet. But over time, it will help your body settle to its natural weight, which is the healthiest weight for you to be.

Other answers:

______________________________________________

______________________________________________

______________________________________________

# Notes

# 7 YOUR HEARING AND SIGHT SENSES

There are two more senses left: your senses of **hearing** (located in your ears) and **sight** (located in your eyes). These can be considered the **school senses**, since they are the ones you use for most of your school learning.

## Your Sense of Hearing

Most young people can hear just fine. But your **sense of hearing** is more than just your ear catching a sound. The brain-body has to be able to make sense of the sound.

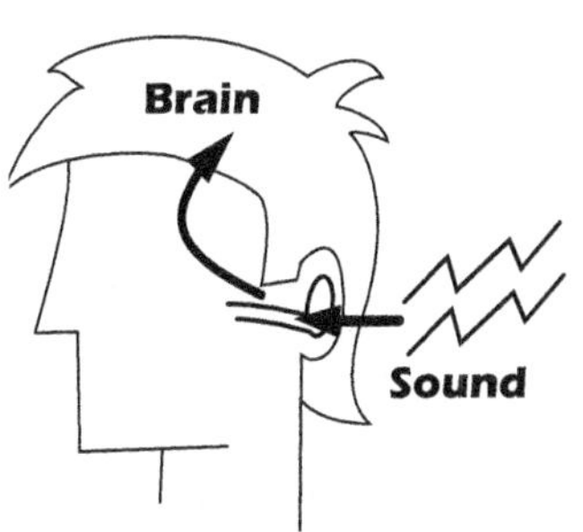


Sometimes the sense of hearing is **over-sensitive**. A person with over-sensitive hearing may not be able to filter out background noises, such as the hum of the lights, the breeze outside the window, the rustling of papers, and the other students whispering to each other.

An **under-sensitive** sense of hearing has a hard time focusing on the teacher at all. It can hear, but it can't tune in and learn.

A strong sense of hearing can filter out these noises and still focus on what the teacher is saying.

## Is your sense of hearing over-sensitive or under-sensitive?

**Part A**

- ☐ When there is noise in the room (such as a ceiling fan moving or lights humming), I get distracted. I can't hear what a person is saying to me.
- ☐ Loud noises really bother me. They hurt, like pain.
- ☐ I tend to hear things that nobody else hears, such as quiet sounds that are supposed to be in the background.
- ☐ I don't like going to the movies because it's too loud.
- ☐ I cover my ears a lot.
- ☐ Certain types of sounds irritate me. If someone's voice is too raspy, nasal, or high-pitched, I have to leave the room.

**Part B**

- ☐ Sometimes I can't tell the difference between similar words when someone says them, such as *bear* and *bore*.
- ☐ I often can't identify someone by their voice.
- ☐ I often forget things people tell me. I remember much better if I see things written down.
- ☐ I often ask the teacher to repeat what he or she just said.
- ☐ I have difficulty singing in tune.
- ☐ I can't always tell what direction a sound comes from.

If you checked off more than 3 items in **Part A**, then you are probably **over-sensitive** in your sense of hearing.

If you checked off more than 3 items in **Part B**, then you are probably **under-sensitive** in your sense of hearing.

### Did you know?

*An owl can hear a mouse stepping on a twig from 75 feet (20 m) away.*

# PLAY IT AGAIN

## Your Sense of Sight

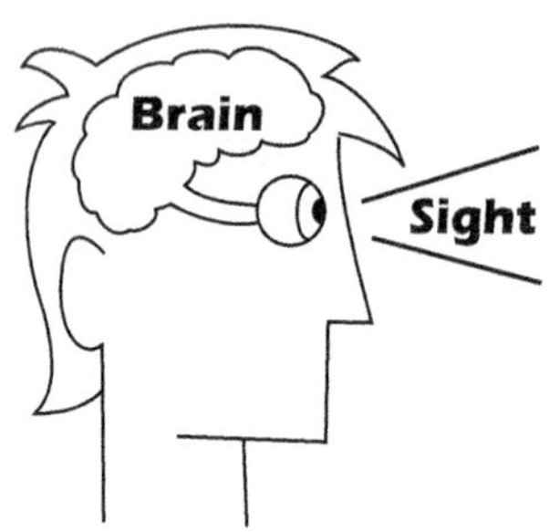


Your **sense of sight** is located in your eyes. The eyes respond to **light** reflected off objects. This light triggers electricity in the back of the eye, which travels to the brain. The brain then has to interpret what the eye saw.

People get most of their information from their eyes. So eyes are very important for learning at school. More than any other sense, our eyes guide us and teach us.

Some people's eyes are **over-sensitive**. This means that the eyes send messages that are too strong to the brain. Bright lights can be painful. It can also mean that the brain reacts to ordinary sight messages too strongly. Either way, seeing things can hurt.

The opposite is a person whose eyes are **under-sensitive**. These people need very bright light and bold, colorful things to look at for their brain to get enough information. If details aren't strong or clear, under-sensitive eyes can't make sense of them.

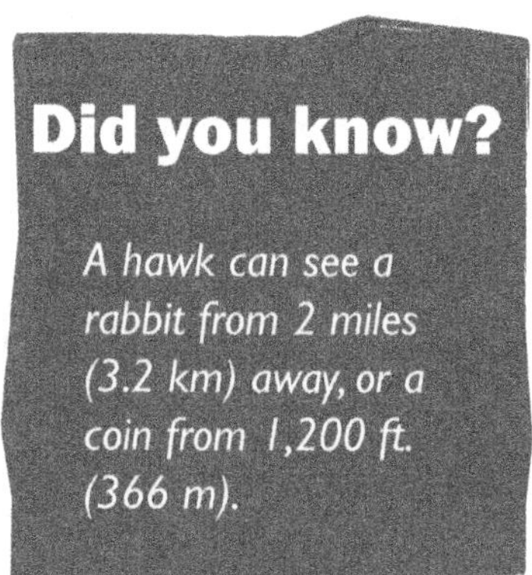

Did you know?
*A hawk can see a rabbit from 2 miles (3.2 km) away, or a coin from 1,200 ft. (366 m).*

## Is your sense of sight over-sensitive or under-sensitive?

**Part A**

- ☐ I don't like bright lights. I have to shield my eyes from the sun.
- ☐ I sometimes see double.
- ☐ I get tired from reading.
- ☐ Sports that have quick movements make me nervous. I can't really see what's going on.
- ☐ I wear sunglasses. I would wear them indoors if I could.
- ☐ The glare of light on a white page makes it hard for me to read.
- ☐ Watching fast-moving objects can make me feel dizzy.
- ☐ Certain types of patterns, shapes, and colors irritate me. I don't like looking at them.

**Part B**

- ☐ I sometimes don't notice signs, even when they are posted right where I usually look.
- ☐ I don't like dim light. I like very bright lights. I look right at bright light.
- ☐ I have difficulty shifting my focus from the blackboard to my notebook and back again.
- ☐ I don't always understand what I'm reading because my eyes start to skim over the words.
- ☐ When I read aloud, I leave out words.
- ☐ I confuse words that look similar, such as *ran* and *run*.
- ☐ I don't cut straight with scissors. I tend to go off the line.
- ☐ I sometimes confuse left and right.

If you checked off more than 4 items in **Part A**, then your sense of sight is probably **over-sensitive**.

If you checked off more than 4 items in **Part B**, then your sense of sight is probably **under-sensitive**.

# Hearing and Sight Senses Team Practice

Many of the following suggestions are **practices** and **accommodations** for over-sensitivity. Many of the activities listed in other chapters are helpful for your senses of hearing and sight. In the meantime, if you are over-sensitive in your eyes or ears, then the easiest way to make your life calmer is to get rid of the things that irritate you the most.

## What a Hearing and Sight Senses Team Practice Can Do for You

- make you more comfortable
- help you feel calm
- gently exercise your hearing and sight senses

## Accommodations and Practices

**Control Background Noise:** *If you find quiet background noise annoying, put some padding under your computer to reduce the hum and vibration. Chew gum to cover up background noises.*

**Use Headphones:** *Headphones can help block out background noise. If you prefer headphones with music, then keep the volume low. Loud music can damage your ears.*

**Use Music for Homework:** *Quiet music keeps your senses awake without distracting you. Experiment with different types of background sound. You can play CDs of ocean waves, nature sounds, or water fountains.*

**Protect Yourself from Bright Light:** *Some people find classroom light (and daylight) too bright. Try sitting in the darkest area where the lights are burnt out. Wear sunglasses, tinted lenses, or a baseball cap.*

**Use Nonflickering Lights:** *Ask your school to put nonflicker fluorescent tubes in your classroom. Avoid old TVs and monitors. Use non-flicker lightbulbs when you do homework.*

**Keep Your Work Area Clean:** *Many people are distracted by things they can see. Remove all clutter from your homework area. Also remove clutter from the walls, such as fluttering blinds and twirling mobiles.*

**Practice Eye Activities:** *Play games with flashlights, fiber optic lights, kaleidoscopes, binoculars, and microscopes. Watch a lava lamp, a fire in a fireplace, or fish swimming in a fish tank. Turn out the lights, wait till your eyes adjust to the darkness, then try to make out the shape of things in the room.*

**Play Aim Games:** *Play bean-bag toss games to help you focus your aim. Play magnetic darts. Trace cartoons using thin tracing paper. (Tape the tracing paper to the page so that you can take breaks.)*

**Join a Band:** *Learn to play a musical instrument. Consider wearing ear plugs or headphones to block out part of the noise for the first while.*

# Notes

## Review
# Hearing and Sight

- Sight and sound are the two **school senses**, since you use them a lot at school.
- An **over-sensitive hearing sense** is distracted by background sounds. An **under-sensitive hearing sense** can't focus on what the teacher is saying.
- An **over-sensitive sense of sight** finds bright lights painful. An **under-sensitive sense of sight** has a hard time seeing details.
- The most important part of sight and sound team practice is to build **accommodations** into your day to reduce irritations.

## Sight and Sound Activity Ideas That Interest Me

____ control background noise

____ use headphones

____ use music for homework

____ protect yourself from bright light

____ use nonflickering lights

____ do eye activities

____ play aim games

____ join music class

________________________

________________________

________________________

## Questions to Consider

**1. If my friend and I both see a color and call it yellow, maybe I really see green, and my friend sees the real yellow. Or maybe neither of us really sees yellow. Is that what this sight sense is all about?**

It's more that you see a hot, painful yellow, and your friend sees a soothing, soft yellow. Both call it yellow, but for one person, it's terrible, and for the other, it's nice.

Other answers:

______________________________

______________________________

______________________________

**2. Won't people think I'm weird if I wear sunglasses in class?**

Many people have to protect their eyes from bright light. You may not have noticed that some students wear sunglasses in class because of eye problems. So people don't really notice. You might also consider getting lightly tinted glasses instead of full sunglasses.

Other answers:

______________________________

______________________________

______________________________

**3. If I am over-sensitive or under-sensitive in my sense of sight, could that affect my ability to read or do math?**

Yes. If your sense of sight is under-sensitive, you might not see all the words or numbers on the page. Your eyes might not stay focused on the page. If they are over-sensitive, they might find the white paper too bright. Or they might get tired very easily. Some people place colored transparencies over their pages to reduce these problems.

Other answers:

______________________________________________

______________________________________________

______________________________________________

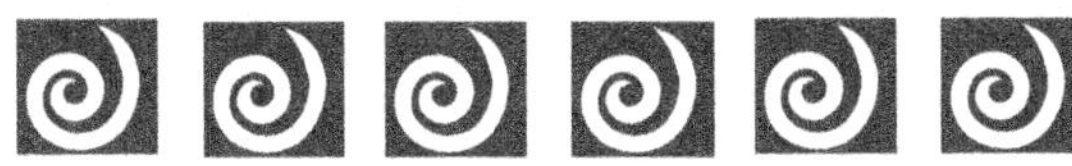

# Notes

# 8 YOUR SENSES AND EMOTIONS

Your **emotions** are linked to your senses because emotions create feelings—we even call them "feelings."

A person can "feel" **anger, surprise, sadness, and joy**. There is a strong physical side to emotions, such as feeling hot and dizzy and turning red when you are embarrassed.

As you grow up, your emotions become more intense. As an adolescent's brain grows, one of the parts that grows most is the **emotion side of your brain**. Just a few short years ago, your main emotions were just the basic ones—fear, happiness, sadness, and surprise. Now you may find that you have a whole new set of emotions—jealousy, desire, love, depression, elation, insecurity, confidence, and so on.

Not only are these emotions new, but they are also much **deeper** than your childhood emotions. Loneliness is much lonelier now. Happiness is wildly happy, and sadness is despair. And embarrassment—well, for many young people, embarrassment can feel really, *really* embarrassing.

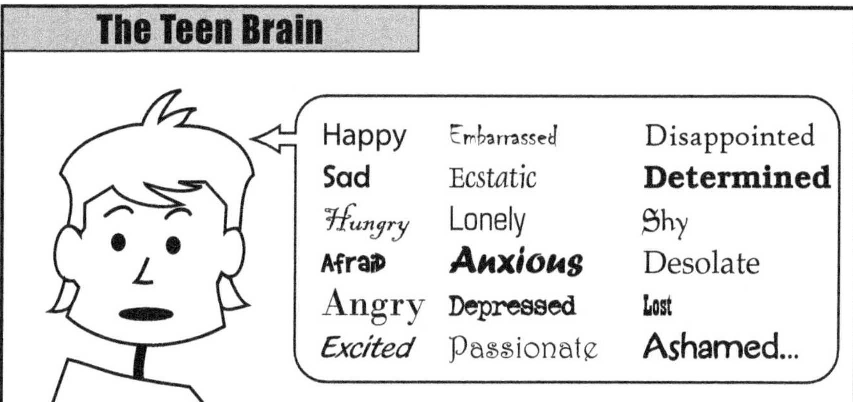


## Did you know?

*A baby rat that does not feel love and cuddling from its mother will have serious health problems. Its body temperature will drop, its heart rate will increase, its breathing will become choppy, it won't sleep, and it won't grow.*

## Pre-teen and Teen Emotions

Every young person is unique, but there are definite patterns to the growth of their emotions during the pre-teen and teen years. Here are some of the characteristics of adolescent emotions.

**Mood Swings:** Everyone says that teens have mood swings. But you aren't really swinging between moods. Your moods just don't have good brakes and volume control. They can suddenly turn up too loud or veer off in a strange direction. You're not in charge of your emotions the way you used to be.

Remember how clumsy you sometimes feel because your arms and legs are growing longer? Your emotions are growing bigger too. You will feel awkward with these bigger, deeper emotions until you've grown into them. Hormones add to mood swings too, because they make you experience bewildering new feelings.

**Constant Change**: Young teens are growing and changing almost by the minute, both in their bodies and in their brains. You may already have zits, new body hair, perspiration odors, voice changes, and growth spurts. And then you are dealing with new school pressures and social pressures. You aren't the same person you were yesterday—and you might even be wondering who you really are. What seemed funny to you yesterday might make you furious today. It's exhausting dealing with the stress of all this emotion all the time.

**Ups and Downs:** The teen years have wild ups and downs. You may feel good about yourself one day and hate yourself the next. You'll think your mom and dad are superheroes one day and space aliens the next. You might find you over-react to small things that people accidentally do to you—or your friends over-react to small things that you do to them. Everything is high drama.

**Everyone Becomes Weird:** You may find that you have difficulty understanding other people's emotions or seeing the world through someone else's eyes. The amount of emotional information you have to deal with just for yourself gets in the way of dealing with other people's emotions at the same time. This means you can end up interpreting things the wrong way.

You may believe that you are a good judge of other people's character. But at the same time, you might find people's behavior very confusing. Fortunately, by the time you are about 18 years old, you will be able to read people much better, and the world will start making more sense.

**Risks Look Like Fun:** Teens sometimes do dangerous things for kicks. This can be a type of sensation-seeking. It can also have to do with feeling emotions so strongly that they sometimes overcome good sense. The desire to fit in and look good might make you do something you know is dangerous.

For teens doing risky activities, their own behavior doesn't make sense to them either. They watch themselves doing something dangerous and still feel unable to stop themselves.

Young people need to become aware of the little voice inside their head that whispers warnings at them. Whenever they agree to do something risky, this little voice tries to get their attention through the emotional blur. It's important to learn to hear that little voice and feel its quiet nudge. Get in the habit of asking yourself: *What is the worst thing that could happen here?* If the answer is something pretty bad, then the risks are too high, and you should go home.

## Do you find emotions overwhelming?

- ☐ I have difficulty taking advice from adults. Advice feels like criticism, even when it makes sense.
- ☐ Some days I get along with my parents. Some days I don't.
- ☐ I have too much to think about almost all the time.
- ☐ Everyone is on my case all the time. That makes me feel moody and irritable.
- ☐ Loneliness is the worst feeling.
- ☐ Some days I feel really good about myself. But then the next day, I feel like a complete loser.
- ☐ Some days I don't believe things are ever going to get any better.
- ☐ People always tell me that I'm insensitive and self-centered, especially my parents. They don't understand that I care.

Strong emotions and confusion are normal parts of the pre-teen and teen years. You are still getting used to the feeling of your new emotions. Some days, these new feelings are very hard to handle. But in time, you will get used to them.

## Grouchy Moods

Your senses are attached to your emotions. So if your senses aren't getting enough stimulation, and your nerve networks are too weak to cope, that will put your brain-body in a **grouchy mood**.

Here are some times when you are likely to feel this grouchiness:

- after you have been on the computer too long. You have been sitting still, and your movement senses are starved for activity.

- after a long day at school. You may have been sitting still, which has made your movement senses edgy. You may have been looking and listening a lot, which has tired out your senses of hearing and sight.
- when you are hungry. If you haven't eaten for a while, or if your last meal was not nutritious, then your brain-body may need food. All your senses will feel lousy.

I'M GROUCHY AND FEELING DOWN. I NEED GUM...
Gum

When you feel yourself falling into a grouchy mood, or when other people start telling you that you are grouchy, grab one of your **mouth tools** or do a **one-minute practice**. You'll start feeling better very quickly. Later, when you have some time by yourself, do one of your **team practices**.

## Crazy Moods

Sometimes you can end up getting too much activity for your senses. Under-sensitive senses can end up demanding too much stimulation all at once. If your nerve networks aren't strong enough to control it, you will end up in a **crazy mood**. When this happens, you will become wild and won't be able to think or control yourself.

Here are some times when you are likely to feel this craziness:

- when you are playing a wild and crazy game. You are enjoying all the fun sensations of running around but can feel yourself losing control.
- when you are eating junk food. All the spicy, sweet, and salty tastes, as well as the low protein, might over-stimulate your mouth senses and make you feel like running and jumping around.
- when people around you are excited and making a lot of noise. You are having fun with them, but all the noise and excitement is getting to be too much. You begin to lose control.
- when you have been sitting still for a long time. You might find that later you can't stop moving.

When you feel yourself falling into a crazy mood, or when people start telling you to cool it or settle down, grab one of your **mouth tools**, or do a **one-minute practice**. After you have calmed down and have a few minutes by yourself, do an activity that you know helps soothe your senses.

I'M TOO BOUNCY AND WILD! I NEED SOME WATER TO CALM DOWN.

# Emotions Team Practice

Remember that the basement of your house is your senses, and your physical activity skills are the first floor. Emotional control is on the second floor. By strengthening the nerve networks of your senses and developing your physical skills, you build up the foundation that supports your emotions. This leaves you calmer and better able to deal with the challenges of being an adolescent.

## What An Emotions Team Practice Can Do for You

- help get **rid of irritations**. When you have less to deal with, you can focus on your social life.
- **keep your brain-body calm**. One-minute practices and mouth tools keep your senses relaxed.
- help you to be **less irritable** with your friends. You spend less time being angry and **more time and energy having fun**.
- give you **more confidence** because you feel calm.
- help you learn that what sometimes feels like emotions is really **your senses calling for action**.
- help you **cope**. Even if irritations build up during the day, you know what to do. You use mouth tools and one-minute practices. You grab quick walks or cold drinks. Instead of blowing up, you blow it away. When you get home, you work off whatever is left, by bouncing, jumping, swinging, or wrestling.

## Team Practice

These activities work the senses most connected to your emotions. They will help you feel calm and relaxed, which will help you deal with your emotions.

**Ball Flop:** *Flop yourself over a fitness ball, forward or backward, stretching your back and arms over the ball. Round yourself to fit the ball. Rock slowly back and forth or lightly bounce the ball beneath your belly.*

**Music:** *Learn to play a solo musical instrument, such as a guitar or a hand drum. The music and rhythm will soothe your hearing, touch, and muscle senses. The music will also let you to express some of your emotions.*

**Resistance Bands:** *Resistance band exercises can help reduce stress. You can buy a resistance band at many pharmacies and home healthcare stores, and they usually come with instructions. After a stressful day, do some slow stretches.*

**Punching Bag:** *If you find you have emotional stress building up inside, get a punching bag. Hang it in the basement and take out your anger on it. You'll build up strength, work your body and gravity senses, and reduce your inner anger. Punching a pillow sometimes works too.*

**Neck Rolls:** *Slowly bring your chin to your chest and hold it there. Then roll it slowly to your right, stopping at the shoulder. Keep your shoulders down on both sides to stretch your neck muscles. Return to the center, then slowly roll to the left.*

**Breathing:** *Slow, deep breathing exercises can be very soothing. Even 15 minutes of slow breathing exercises leaves a person feeling calm and refreshed all day. You can learn these breathing exercises from videos, tapes, or books.*

**Safe Places:** *Have a safe space both at home and at school where you can go to get emotional rest. It should be a quiet place where nothing happens. You might find after just a few minutes of quiet, your emotions calm right down. At home, you might add a certain kind of lighting or music, a favorite chair, or a calming smell.*

**Recess:** *Middle schools and high schools don't usually have recesses and playgrounds. Yet growing brain-bodies need activity breaks during the day to reduce stress from sitting too long, working at computers, and dealing with too many people. So give yourself recess. If the school rules permit it, take a quick walk outside with a friend.*

**Nutrition:** *Many younger teens experience mood swings because of blood sugar crashes and poor nutrition. Eating more fresh fruits, vegetables, and proteins, and reducing sugars and starches can even out your moods and make you feel happier.*

**Daily Sensory Team Practices:** *If your senses are irritable, then your emotions aren't going to feel good. A daily sensory warm-up every morning and afternoon and three sensory team practices every week will keep your senses feeling good. You will feel happier and less edgy.*

# Notes

## Review Your Emotions

- Emotions cause feelings, which come from the senses.
- **Teen emotions** are very strong because a lot of them are new.
- If your senses are not getting enough activity and stimulation, then you might go into a **grouchy mood**.
- If your senses get too much activity and stimulation, you might go into a **crazy mood**.
- **Regular sensory team practices** will help keep your emotions calm by strengthening your nerve networks.

## Emotion Activity Ideas That Interest Me

____ ball flop

____ music

____ resistance bands

____ punching bag

____ neck rolls

____ breathing

____ safe places

____ recess

____ nutrition

____ sensory team practices

________________________

________________________

## Questions to Consider

**1. Why are the emotions linked to the senses?**

The feelings of emotions are caused by your senses. For example, when you are afraid, you can feel your heart thumping hard. Your face feels tight or sweaty, and your insides feel kind of sick. Although the emotions can't create their own sensations, they create them through your senses.

Other answers:

________________________________________

________________________________________

________________________________________

**2. When I'm in a grouchy mood, I don't want to do anything or listen to anybody. I just want to be alone. I can't do exercises then.**

This is a perfect time to use a mouth tool. Make sure you always have your best mouth tools handy. Even when people are grouchy, they usually can't resist a tasty goody to chew, suck, or crunch on. You'll feel much better afterward.

Other answers:

________________________________________

________________________________________

________________________________________

**3. I blow up a lot. My brain seems to get stuck, and I then can't think. I start pounding, yelling, and making things worse. Sensory team practices won't help me in these situations.**

The brain can get stuck when strong emotions and sensations rush to your brain all at once. Your brain can't deal with them all. They jam your nerve networks and your brain so that you can't think. Regular sensory team practices will help keep your brain from getting stuck. If your nerve networks are strong from regular practice, and if senses are calm, then your emotions and sensations will flow smoothly to and from your brain. You'll have a better chance of thinking in these situations.

Other answers:

________________________________________

________________________________________

________________________________________

# Notes

# 9

# YOUR SENSES AND SOCIAL LIFE

*Social* refers to friendship and being with other people. To be happy, most young people need to be happy in their social life. And to do this, they need to be able to make and keep friends.

You need to be able to use your brain in social situations. If your brain-body is overwhelmed by your senses and emotions, then it can't learn how to interact with others. But if your nerve networks are strong, then your brain-body will have the time and energy to manage your social life.

As a young person, you probably attend a middle school or high school. The social scene there might be very intense. You'll need have a clear mind to be able to manage it well.

## Your Social World

Being an adolescent is about school and friends. Middle schools and high schools are full of young people trying out their personalities on others. You are probably one of them.

Here are some suggestions for making your social experiences better.

## Groups and Status

A lot of young teens try to be cool and hang out with the in-crowd because they want **status**. Many want to have cool status or sporty status. Most want more status than they already have. It seems you can never have enough status in the pre-teen and teen social world.

Status is like power. But it's is a very shaky kind of power, because it depends on who you associate with, not on who you are. People who seek friends for status often don't have real friends. So having even one or two real friends is better than having a lot of status friends who are only there to look good.

## Teasing and Bullying

Teasing and bullying are often a part of everyday life for people with sensory issues. Strength, sportiness, co-ordination, good looks, and smooth social skills are the cold hard cash of the adolescent world—they get you where you want to go. Pre-teens and teens who lack these skills don't have much power, and they often have to put up with teasing.

Don't assume that people who tease are mean. Sometimes they aren't teasing at all—they're just joking around. Other times, they are teasing in a gentle way, not trying to be mean to you.

If the teasing seems to be mean, maybe it's because the other person is nervous about differences. When people don't understand something, they sometimes poke and prod, often very unkindly. Sometimes the easiest way to get rid of teasing is to find a way to explain things. You don't need to tell your life story—just give them enough information to get the picture. Working in a compliment or two also helps.

If you find you don't know how to handle it well, make an appointment to talk to a guidance counsellor to get suggestions.

**Did you know?**

Many pre-teens and teens socialize through social media (internet). They have a real life and an online life. Some experts think this is because young people don't have much freedom in real life, but online, they can experience freedom of expression.

## ★ FIRST DAY IN THE GYM ★

Matt decides to try out the weight machines.
HM, I WONDER WHAT I DO...

Ow!!
Ha ha ha!

He asks for help... and works in a compliment.
YOU LOOK LIKE YOU KNOW WHAT YOU'RE DOING...
Compliment
COULD YOU SHOW ME HOW TO DO THIS?

Most people like to show off a little. So Matt gets a free lesson... and some respect.
SURE THING! YOU'VE ALMOST GOT IT!


### Your Habits

Do you have quirky habits? You may have developed unusual ways of dealing with sensory difficulties. For example, you might play computer games all the time because it allows you to avoid sensation. But computer games are a bit anti-social, especially if there are people around that you could be talking to. Online friendships are lame compared to real-life friendships.

You may also have developed habits such as playing with your hair because it irritates your neck. This would be a time to get a new hair style.

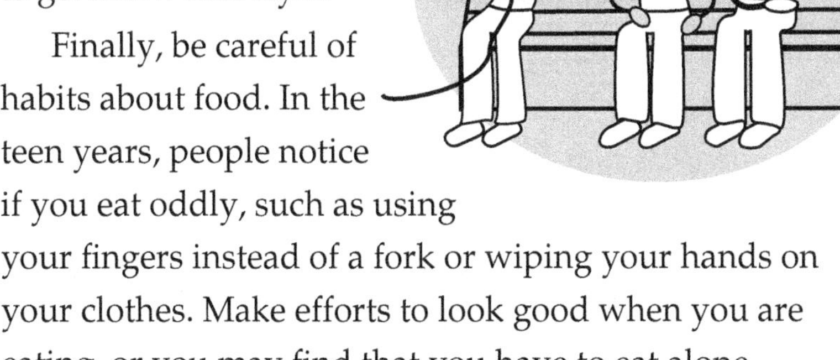


Finally, be careful of habits about food. In the teen years, people notice if you eat oddly, such as using your fingers instead of a fork or wiping your hands on your clothes. Make efforts to look good when you are eating, or you may find that you have to eat alone.

## Making Friends

Being successful in the social world is a goal of many adolescents. Success means that you have a pleasant personality that many people like.

To *have* a friend, you have to *be* a friend. This means **not thinking about friends as things to have or get**. Don't expect others to give their friendship to you. You should give your friendship to them.

Teens who have a lot of friends probably don't need

your friendship. But there are always teens who don't have many friends.These friends won't be the coolest people, and they won't get you cool status. But that will make it easier to hang out with them, because they will have fewer expectations.

If you are patient and accepting of their differences, they will end up being patient and accepting of yours. You need friends who don't care if you wear sunglasses indoors, or wear a sweater when nobody else does, or if you aren't very good at sports. They'll be open to doing some of the things you like to do if you are open to doing some of the things they like to do.

It's almost an unwritten rule in middle and high school that you are supposed to want to be cool. But you have to decide if that's something you really want. If not, then don't pretend it's important to you.

# Social Team Practice

Remember that senses are the basement of your brain-body house, physical activities are on the first floor, and emotions are on the second floor. Social behavior is up in the attic, and it depends on the strength of all the floors beneath it. Regular sensory team workouts build up the foundation for a happier, friendlier you.

## What a Social Team Practice Can Do For You

- help make you more calm and less fidgety. You'll find it **easier to sit and talk with others.**
- help remove irritations from your life so that you have less to worry about. You'll be able to **watch, listen, and fit in** with your friends.
- help you listen and pay attention in class. You'll have less homework and **more time for friends.**
- help make you **less bouncy and silly**. It will be easier for your friends to be with you.
- help you feel **in control of your brain-body**. You will know how to use snack practices and mouth tools.
- help you to be less worried and anxious. You will feel **more like trying new social activities.**
- help you eat more foods. You will have more confidence about **social activities involving food.**
- help you meet **new friends** through new activities.
- teach you **who you really are.**

## Team Practice

**Daily Sensory Team Practices:** *Sensory team practices and warm-ups will keep your sensory networks strong. With a strong basement, your brain-body will be able to cope with your social world.*

**School Musical:** *Join the set-building team for your school's musical. The hammering, painting, and heavy work is a sensory team practice. Meanwhile, you will make new friends and feel involved in a big school project.*

**School Band:** *Join the school band. You will go on band trips and other activities. At the same time, your instrument will provide a sensory team practice for your muscle, mouth, touch, and hearing senses.*

**Fundraising:** *Many youth organizations do fundraising projects and need volunteers. Collecting canned food and baking for a bake sale will help you meet new friends while doing a sensory team practice.*

**Outings:** *Call up new friends to go skating, biking, sledding, or hiking. You can talk while you move and combine friendship with a sensory team practice. Afterward, go to a restaurant and order one of your best mouth tools.*

**Recess:** *During breaks in your school day, invite a friend to go for a walk or play one-on-one in an empty gym. This will wake up your senses for the rest of the day while helping you get to know someone better.*

# Review Your Soci

- Your senses affect your social life because the brain-body needs to be calm and confident to be able to think in social situations.
- School can be challenging because of **groups, status, teasing, and bullying**.
- You can improve your social life by improving your **social habits** and making efforts to make and keep **friends**.
- Sensory team practices help you become a more social person.
- Social team practices are sensory team activities that you do with other people.

## Social Activity Ideas That Interest Me

____ sensory team practices ______________________________

____ school musical ______________________________

____ school band ______________________________

____ fundraising ______________________________

____ outings ______________________________

____ recess ______________________________

# YOUR TEAM, YOUR LIFE

You've read about a lot of new ideas in this book. You've learned about your two movement senses:

- your **gravity** sense
- your **muscle** sense

And you've learned about your five feeling senses:

- your sense of **touch**
- your mouth senses: **taste** and **smell** (and touch)
- your sense of **hearing** and **sight**

You also learned about two other parts of your life that are linked to your senses:

- your **emotions**
- your **social life**

Hopefully you've tried several of the practice and warm-up activities. Maybe by now you are already doing one-minute practices and using mouth tools in your day-to-day life. Now it's time to put all the pieces together so that you have a coaching plan that works for you.

Go back through the book and collect some ideas for sensory team practices. Choose the activities you already like and some you would like to try.

Make sure that the activities you choose fit together. Have a mix of different types of activities so that they fit into your schedule.

## Scheduled Activities

Scheduled activities are activities that you sign up for and have to go to at a specific time every week.

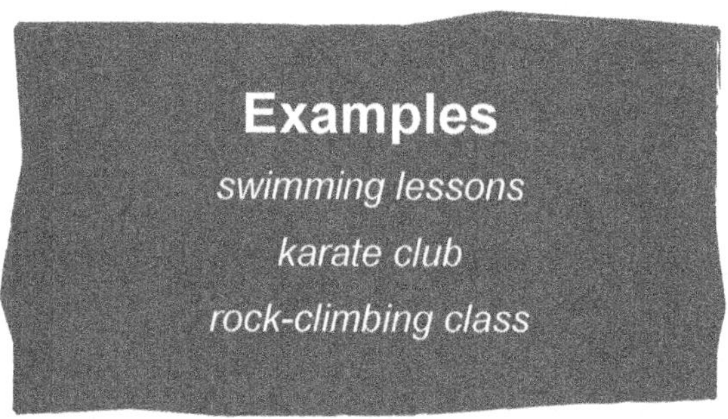

Examples
swimming lessons
karate club
rock-climbing class


Do one for now, but gradually work up to two or three.

___

___

___

___

___

___

___

___

___

___

## Embedded Activities

Embedded activities are activities that are part of your daily routine, especially for school days. You don't need to plan these activities because they are just part of your day.

**Examples**

*walking to school*

*gym at lunch*

*trampoline when you get home.*

Do two or three for now, till you get used to them, then add more.

## Social Activities

Social activities are activities you do with friends.

**Examples**

*cycling with a friend on Saturdays*

*set-building for the school play*

*playing badminton*

Do at least one every day, but work up to two or three.

## Quickie Activities

Quickie activities are one-minute practices and mouth tools that work for you.

**Examples**

*chair push-ups*

*walking on tiptoe*

*chewing gum*

*drinking water from a spout bottle*

List the ones that have worked for you. Keep all your mouth tools handy.

## Accommodations

Accommodations are changes you make to your life so that you can be more comfortable.

**Examples**

*wearing sunglasses*

*sitting on a fitness ball*

List accommodations that have worked for you. You will want to use all of them.

______________________________________________

______________________________________________

______________________________________________

______________________________________________

______________________________________________

______________________________________________

______________________________________________

______________________________________________

______________________________________________

______________________________________________

______________________________________________

______________________________________________

## Your Team, Your Life

Use the activities you listed and those you checked off in the chapters to create a coaching plan for yourself.

- What will your days be like? How will they start?
- What will you do in the morning? In the afternoon? In the evening? On weekends?
- How will you deal with clothes? Food? Family? Schoolwork?
- How will you make time for friends while keeping up with your sensory team practices?
- What does your team need every day? Every week?

On the next page is an example of one person's coaching plan.

## My Team, My Life

My team needs 10 minutes of jumping on a mini trampoline before breakfast.

My team needs a breakfast of whole grains, fruits, nuts, and meats. Lunch is a nutritious sandwich and fruit. Dinner includes a healthy salad.

My team needs food to be mildly flavored. But I experiment with new tastes in small doses all the time.

My team needs a spout bottle of water on my desk at school so that I can sip on it whenever I feel restless.

My team needs hand and finger stretches before I write. Since pencils break easily and are hard to sharpen, I use mechanical pencils. I carry a mini laptop for taking long notes.

My team needs a foam pad under my computer to absorb the hum. My monitor is no-flicker, and the contrast is turned down. A fitness ball is my desk chair.

My team needs quick stretch breaks throughout the day to keep my muscles awake so that I can concentrate.

My team needs a walk to the park with a friend during lunch hour.

My team needs a hand fidget to help me pay attention whenever I have to sit still. I carry it in my pencil case.

My team needs two evenings of exercise: swimming on Tuesdays and karate class on Thursdays.

My team needs quiet music while I eat supper.

My team needs dancing to hip-hop music in the basement after supper. Nobody is allowed to come downstairs till I'm done.

My team needs me to keep gum in my pocket whenever I go to the movies because the darkness, bright lights, and loud noises can make me feel nervous.

My team needs lemonade or fig bars to get rid of stress.

My team needs bed sheets that are 100% cotton and clothes that have been washed many times before I wear them.

My team needs fun time with friends. I invite friends over to play games every weekend. I don't focus on winning, just on having fun.

Now you try it. Write down your ideas. Plan what your team needs. Create a life that works for you.

## My Team, My Life

My team needs ______________________________

My team needs ______________________________

My team needs ______________________________

My team needs ______________________________

My team needs ______________________________

My team needs ______________________________

My team needs ______________________________

My team needs ____________________________________________

______________________________________________________________

______________________________________________________________

My team needs ____________________________________________

______________________________________________________________

______________________________________________________________

My team needs ____________________________________________

______________________________________________________________

______________________________________________________________

My team needs ____________________________________________

______________________________________________________________

______________________________________________________________

My team needs ____________________________________________

______________________________________________________________

______________________________________________________________

My team needs ____________________________________________

______________________________________________________________

______________________________________________________________

My team needs ____________________________________________

______________________________________________________________

______________________________________________________________

My team needs ____________________________________________

______________________________________________________________

## Summary

Coach ______________________________

My best gravity activities:

______________________________

______________________________

______________________________

My best muscle activities:

______________________________

______________________________

______________________________

My best touch activities:

______________________________

______________________________

______________________________

My best mouth tools:

______________________________

______________________________

______________________________

My best accommodations (touch, sight, sound):

________________________________________

________________________________________

________________________________________

Best things to do when I feel grouchy, tired, and down:

________________________________________

________________________________________

________________________________________

Best things to do when I feel crazy, wired, and out of control:

________________________________________

________________________________________

________________________________________

My best strategies for making and keeping friends:

________________________________________

________________________________________

________________________________________

## Your Gravity Sense

## Your Muscle Sense

## Your Touch Sense

## Your Mouth Sense

## Your Sight and Hearing Senses

## Your Senses and Emotions

## Your Senses and Social Life

# RESOURCES

## Occupational Therapy Associations

### Australia

*Australian Association of Occupational Therapists*
6/340 Gore Street
Fitzroy, Victoria, 3065
Telephone: 03-9415-2900
Website: www.ausot.com.au

### Canada

*Canadian Association of Occupational Therapists*
CTTC Building, Suite 3400
1125 Colonel By Drive
Ottawa ON K1S 5R1
Telephone: 613-523-2268
Website: www.caot.ca

### Ireland

*Association of Occupational Therapists of Ireland*
Ground Floor Office, Bow Bridge House
Kilmainham
Dublin 8
Telephone: 01 6337222
Website: www.aoti.ie

### New Zealand

*New Zealand Association of Occupational Therapists*
Level 1, Red Cross House
69 Molesworth Street, Thorndon
PO Box 12-506
Wellington 6144
Telephone: 644-473-6510
Website: www.nzaot.com

## South Africa

*Occupational Therapy Association of South Africa*
PO Box 11695
Hatfield, 0028
Telephone: 27-(0)12-362-5457
Website: www.otasa.org.za

## United Kingdom

*British Association/College of Occupational Therapists*
106-114 Borough High Street
Southwark
London SE1 1LB
Telephone: 020-7357-6480
Website: www.cot.org.uk

## United States

*The American Occupational Therapy Association*
4720 Montgomery Lane
PO Box 31220
Bethesda, MD 20824-1220
Telephone: 301-652-2682
Website: www.aota.org

# Web Resources

### SPD Australia
www.spdaustralia.com

### SPD Foundation
www.spdfoundation.net

### SPD Canada
www.spdcanada.org

### Sensory Integration Network, UK and Ireland
www.sensoryintegration.org.uk

### Sensory Processing Disorder Resource Center
www.sensory-processing-disorder.com

### Sensory Smarts
www.sensorysmarts.com

# Good Books

Auer, Christopher, and Susan Blumberg. *Parenting a Child with Sensory Processing Disorder.* New Harbinger, 2006.

Ayres, Jean A., Philip R. Erwin, and Zoe Mailloux. *Love, Jean.* Crestport Press, 2004.

Biel, Lindsey, and Nancy Peske. *Raising a Sensory Smart Child.* Penguin, 2005.

Eide, Brock, and Fernette Eide. *The Mislabeled Child.* Hyperion, 2006.

Greene, Ross W. *The Explosive Child.* HarperCollins, 2005.

Henry, Diana. *Sensory Integration Tools for Teens.* HenryOT, 2004.

Heller, Sharon. *Too Loud, Too Bright, Too Fast, Too Tight.* HarperCollins, 2002.

Koomar, Jane, Carol Kranoqitz, Lynn Balzer-Martin, Elizabeth Haber, and Deanna Iris Sava. *Answers to Questions Teachers Ask About Sensory Integration.* Future Horizons, 2001.

Kranowitz, Carol Stock. *The Out-of-Sync Child.* Perigee, 1998.

Kranowitz, Carol Stock. *The Goodenoughs Get in Sync.* Sensory Resources, 2008.

Mauro, Terri, and Sharon A. Cermak. *The Everything Parent's Guide to Sensory Integration.* Adams Media, 2006.

McGraw, Jay. *Life Strategies for Teens.* Fireside, 2000.

Miller, Lucy Jane, and Doris A. Fuller. *Sensational Kids.* Perigee, 2007.

Renna, Diane M. *Meghan's World: The Story of One Girl's Triumph over Sensory Processing Disorder.* Indigo Impressions, 2007.

Veenendall, Jennifer. *Arnie and his School Tools: Simple Sensory Solutions that Build Success.* Autism Asperger Publishing Company, 2008.